# FOOD&WINE

# quick from scratch
# *italian* cookbook

# FOOD&WINE

**EDITOR** Judith Hill
**ASSOCIATE EDITOR** Susan Lantzius Rich
**ASSISTANT EDITOR** Laura Byrne Russell
**EDITORIAL ASSISTANT** Evette Manners
**MANAGING EDITOR** Terri Mauro
**COPY EDITOR** Barbara A. Mateer
**WINE EDITOR** Steve Miller
**ART DIRECTOR** Nina Scerbo
**PHOTOGRAPHER** Melanie Acevedo
**FOOD STYLIST** Rori Trovato
**PROP STYLIST** Robyn Glaser
**FOOD STYLIST FOR PHOTOGRAPHS ON PP. 61, 75** Roscoe Betsill
**PROP STYLIST FOR PHOTOGRAPHS ON PP. 61, 75** Denise Canter

**V.P., BOOKS & PRODUCTS/PUBLISHER** Marshall Corey
**DIRECTOR, BOOK PROGRAMS** Bruce Spanier
**SENIOR MARKETING MANAGER, BRANDED BOOKS** Eric Lucie
**ASSISTANT MARKETING MANAGER** Lizabeth Clark
**DIRECTOR OF FULFILLMENT & PREMIUM VALUE** Phil Black
**MANAGER OF CUSTOMER EXPERIENCE & PRODUCT DEVELOPMENT** Charles Graver
**DIRECTOR OF FINANCE** Thomas Noonan
**ASSOCIATE BUSINESS MANAGER** Desiree Bernardez

**ON THE COVER** Spaghetti with Tomatoes, Basil, Olives and Fresh Mozzarella, P. 52

Copyright © 2009 American Express Publishing Corporation
Published by American Express Publishing
1120 Avenue of the Americas
New York, New York 10036

ISBN 13: 978-1-60320-076-9
ISBN 10: 1-60320-076-2
Library of Congress Control Number: 2009928259

If you would like to order any of our hardcover Collector's Edition books, please call us at 1-800-284-4145 (Monday through Friday, 7:00 a.m.— 12:00 a.m., or Saturday and Sunday, 7:00 a.m.— 10:00 p.m. Central Time).

PRINTED IN THE UNITED STATES OF AMERICA

AMERICAN EXPRESS
PUBLISHING CORPORATION

**PRESIDENT/C.E.O.** Ed Kelly
**S.V.P./CHIEF MARKETING OFFICER** Mark V. Stanich
**C.F.O./S.V.P./CORPORATE DEVELOPMENT & OPERATIONS** Paul B. Francis
**V.P./GENERAL MANAGERS** Frank Bland, Keith Strohmeier

**PUBLISHER** Richard Fraiman
**GENERAL MANAGER** Steven Sandonato
**EXECUTIVE DIRECTOR, MARKETING SERVICES** Carol Pittard
**DIRECTOR, RETAIL & SPECIAL SALES** Tom Mifsud
**DIRECTOR, NEW PRODUCT DEVELOPMENT** Peter Harper
**ASSISTANT DIRECTOR, BOOKAZINE MARKETING** Laura Adam
**ASSISTANT PUBLISHING DIRECTOR, BRAND MARKETING** Joy Butts
**ASSOCIATE COUNSEL** Helen Wan
**ASSOCIATE MANAGER, PRODUCT MARKETING** Nina Fleishman
**BOOK PRODUCTION MANAGER** Susan Chodakiewicz
**DESIGN & PREPRESS MANAGER** Anne-Michelle Gallero

**SPECIAL THANKS**
Christine Austin, Glenn Buonocore, Jim Childs, Rose Cirrincione, Jacqueline Fitzgerald, Lauren Hall, Jennifer Jacobs, Suzanne Janso, Brynn Joyce, Mona Li, Robert Marasco, Amy Migliaccio, Brooke Reger, Dave Rozzelle, Ilene Schreider, Adriana Tierno, Alex Voznesenskiy, Sydney Webber

## NICE KERN, LLC

**ART DIRECTOR** Patricia Sanchez
**COPY EDITOR** Lisa Leventer
**EDITORIAL ASSISTANT** Zoe Singer
**INDEXER** Elizabeth Parson

# FOOD&WINE

# quick from scratch
# italian cookbook

FOOD&WINE
BOOKS

# CONTENTS

# *faster, better, easier*
# TEST-KITCHEN TIPS

## *Portion sizes*

A traditional Italian dinner includes a number of courses, each offering a moderate portion, as opposed to one large main dish. The first course is usually soup, pasta or rice followed by a fish, chicken or meat second course, often accompanied by vegetables. Salad comes after the second course. Although antipasti and dessert appear at more lavish, special-occasion meals, for everyday dinners antipasti is often skipped and dessert is usually fresh or simply cooked fruit.

With busy workdays and conflicting schedules, Italians and Americans alike often do not have enough time to enjoy a leisurely multicourse meal. We've developed this book with that in mind, and so all of our recipes (excluding antipasti and desserts) are meant to serve as a main dish for four people—even the soups, pasta and rice dishes.

If you'd like to use the recipes to host a more traditional Italian meal for your family or friends, start with an antipasto or several of them; choose a first course from the soup, pasta or rice chapter; follow it with a chicken, meat or fish recipe; and end the meal with one of our delicious, easy Italian desserts. In this case, the first-course recipes will serve six.

## *Quick no-cook antipasti*

You can put together an impressive antipasti platter in minutes with a few choice deli items and pantry staples. Serve the antipasti as an appetizer or even as an informal meal.

**CURED MEATS**—thin slices of prosciutto, coppa, *soppressata*, hard salami or other dried sausages

**CHEESES**—shaved Parmigiano-Reggiano or Asiago, wedges of goat cheese, balls of fresh mozzarella marinated in olive oil and herbs, slices of Taleggio or provolone

**OTHER POSSIBILITIES**—green or black olives, canned tuna, sliced or grated raw vegetables dressed with olive oil, pickled vegetables (*giardiniera*), sliced melon or figs

## *Soup too thick?*

Many Italian-style soups are so chock-full of rice or pasta that much of the liquid is absorbed before the soup hits the table. To thin the soup before serving, simply stir in some extra broth or water. Taste the soup and add more salt and pepper if necessary.

## *Pasta cooking tips*

**COOK PASTA IN LOTS OF BOILING, SALTED WATER.** Count on using at least three quarts of water and one and a half tablespoons of salt to cook three-quarters of a pound of pasta.

**WHEN THE WATER BOILS, ADD THE PASTA ALL AT ONCE AND STIR.** Don't break long strands of pasta in half to make them fit, just ease them in slowly. Stir the pasta frequently as it cooks.

**BEFORE DRAINING THE PASTA, LADLE OUT SOME OF THE COOKING WATER** to save in case the sauce is too thick. Pasta-cooking water thins a sauce and adds a bit of flavor at the same time.

**COOKING TIMES FOR PASTA ARE MERELY GUIDELINES.** To check for doneness, bite into a piece of pasta. It should be slightly chewy. Look at the center of the bitten piece; there should be no opaque white core. Retest frequently.

**DRAIN THE PASTA AND IMMEDIATELY TOSS IT WITH THE SAUCE.** Never rinse pasta unless you're serving it cold, as in a salad, or letting it stand a while undressed, as when constructing lasagna.

## Reviving Parmesan cheese

If a wedge of Parmesan is drying out, wrap it in a damp paper towel and then in plastic wrap or aluminum foil. Refrigerate. A day later, remove the paper towel, rewrap tightly and store in the refrigerator.

## Making risotto

Perfectly cooked risotto is not at all difficult to make; you just need to keep a few important tips in mind.

**USE SHORT- OR MEDIUM-GRAIN RICE;** arborio is the easiest to find.

**STIR THE RICE IN HOT FAT UNTIL IT'S WELL COATED** before adding any liquid to the pan.

**ADD HOT LIQUID TO THE RICE A LITTLE AT A TIME;** don't add more until the previous addition is absorbed.

**KEEP THE LIQUID AT A SIMMER** and stir the rice often.

**THE AMOUNT OF LIQUID YOU NEED TO COOK THE RICE MAY DIFFER** slightly from the amount called for in a recipe. Adjust the quantity if necessary to cook the rice and have some thickened liquid left as a sauce.

## The fish and cheese taboo

Although there are exceptions to every rule (and we make a few of them), fish and cheese are rarely served together in Italy. In fact, fish is seldom combined with any dairy product. To top shrimp risotto with Parmesan, for example, would be considered a heresy.

## Cooking vegetables, Italian style

Italy grows arguably the best produce in the world, and fresh, seasonal vegetables are a mainstay of the Italian diet. When cooking them, Italians do not hold crunchiness as a goal. They cook vegetables until they're tender (but not overcooked) so the flavor reaches its peak.

## Dressing salads

While a perfectly emulsified vinaigrette is important in classic French cuisine, the Italian salad is slightly more relaxed. Simply put the lettuce in a serving bowl, toss with extra-virgin olive oil, salt and pepper, and then toss again with the vinegar. Taste a piece of lettuce and adjust any seasonings.

## Storing fresh basil

Basil leaves have a tendency to turn black quickly in the refrigerator. To make the herb last longer, store a bunch in a jar with enough water to cover the stem ends or roots and then put a plastic bag over the leaves. Or wrap a wet paper towel around the bottom of the bunch and then cover the entire thing with plastic wrap and refrigerate.

## Beloved bread

Italians rarely waste even a single crumb of bread. To recycle bread the Italian way, grill day-old slices for bruschetta; fry cubes in oil with garlic for croutons; run leftover bread in the food processor with the regular blade to make fresh bread crumbs; or toast the fresh bread crumbs in the oven and process them again to make fine dry bread crumbs.

# ITALIAN WINES

| | type | wine | description | food affinity |
|---|---|---|---|---|
| **WHITE** | Light, crisp, neutral | Gavi<br>Orvieto<br>Pinot grigio<br>Soave<br>Verdicchio | *Light body and delicate flavor with good acidity. Made to highlight food, not conflict. Flavors include floral, herbal, nutty and subtle apple notes.* | *Light fish and chicken dishes. Salads. Can handle light tomato sauces.* |
| | Medium, fruity | Chardonnay<br>Pinot bianco<br>Sauvignon blanc<br>Vernaccia di San Gimignano | *Richer and fuller with more obvious fruit flavor. Chardonnay is more spicy, while sauvignon blanc and vernaccia are more herbal or nutty.* | *Richer fish and chicken dishes. Veal. Salads. More highly spiced and herbed foods. Be careful with chardonnay: It is often oaky and can overpower many foods.* |
| | Full, rich | Fiano di Avellino<br>Gewürztraminer<br>Greco di Tufo<br>Tocai friulano | *Full-bodied wines that can overpower a subtle dish. Earthy, nutty, honey and spicy flavors.* | *Rich full-flavored fish, chicken, veal and pork dishes.* |
| **ROSÉ** | Medium, fruity | Lacryma Christi | *Full-bodied with delicate strawberry and earthy flavors.* | *Garlicky and salty foods. Seafood with tomato sauce. Smoked meats; prosciutto.* |
| **RED** | Light, fruity | Bardolino<br>Chianti<br>Dolcetto d'Asti<br>Grignolino<br>Valpolicella | *Simple, grapey, high-acid wines for everyday drinking.* | *Pasta with tomato sauce. Pizza. Chicken. Light-flavored red-meat dishes.* |
| | Medium, rich | Barbera<br>Carmignano<br>Chianti Riserva<br>Dolcetto d'Alba<br>Franciacorta<br>Montepulciano d'Abruzzo<br>Refosco<br>Rosso di Montalcino<br>Salice Salentino<br>Valtellina | *More substantial wines with subtle fruitiness and some earthy and herbal flavors. Moderately tannic.* | *Rich tomato sauce. Pork, veal and red meats. Braised poultry and meats. Stews.* |
| | Full, rich, complex | Barbaresco<br>Barolo<br>Brunello<br>Vino Nobile di Montepulciano | *Italy's most revered wines. Powerful; structured for long-term development with complex, multidimensional flavors.* | *Should be showcased by serving with simply prepared red meat, such as steaks, chops and roasts.* |

# ITALIAN CHEESES

| texture | cheese | milk | description |
|---|---|---|---|
| Soft curd | **Ricotta** | SHEEP'S, WATER BUFFALO'S OR GOAT'S (ITALY); COW'S (U.S.) | *Produced from the whey left over from cheesemaking. Mild in flavor and relatively low in fat. The original Italian version has a drier texture than that produced in the United States.* |
| Soft | **Mascarpone** | COW'S | *Lusciously rich, much like French crème fraîche or English clotted cream. Delicate flavor lends itself graciously to either savory or sweet dishes.* |
| Semisoft | **Gorgonzola** | COW'S | *One of the great blue cheeses of the world. Blue-green veined, full flavored and creamy in texture. There are two types: Sweet is softer and milder tasting; aged is a bit firmer and bolder flavored.* |
| | **Mozzarella** | WATER BUFFALO'S OR GOAT'S (ITALY); COW'S (U.S.) | *Fresh mozzarella has a mild, milky taste and is available salted, unsalted and smoked. Fairly soft texture but not rubbery like that made by big manufacturers.* |
| | **Taleggio** | COW'S | *Square in shape. Full flavored and buttery when ripe. It doesn't quite run when cut into; it bulges.* |
| Semifirm | **Fontina** | COW'S | *Italian fontina is a marvelous melting cheese, with a distinctive nutty taste. Scandinavian fontina is okay, but not exceptional.* |
| Firm | **Asiago** | COW'S | *Mild in flavor. As it ages and hardens, it develops more of a bite and is good for grating.* |
| | **Provolone** | COW'S | *Mild mannered at first. Sharper flavored with age, becoming quite provocative after about a year.* |
| Hard | **Parmigiano-Reggiano** | COW'S | *Real Parmigiano-Reggiano is aged for at least fourteen months and has its name stamped on the rind. Avoid any imposters in a canister.* |
| | **Pecorino Romano** | SHEEP'S (ITALY); COW'S (U.S.) | *Great grating cheese, often substituted for Parmesan. Sharp, intense, relatively salty flavor. The Italian sheep's cheese is fuller and more distinctive.* |

SHRIMP MARINATED IN LEMON
AND OLIVE OIL, P. 20

# *antipasti*

# roasted peppers with caper dressing

*A plate of red and yellow bell peppers tossed with a tangy dressing pleases both the eye and the palate. You can use peppers of only one color, if you prefer, or include an orange and a green bell pepper for a truly spectacular effect.*

**COOK TIME**
15 MINUTES

**SERVES 4**

 2   red bell peppers
 2   yellow bell peppers
 ½   teaspoon lemon juice
 ¾   teaspoon anchovy paste
1½   teaspoons wine vinegar
 ¾   teaspoon salt
 ¼   teaspoon fresh-ground
      black pepper
 ¼   cup olive oil
 2   tablespoons drained
      capers

**1.** Roast the peppers over a gas flame or grill or broil them, turning with tongs, until charred all over, about 10 minutes. When the peppers are cool enough to handle, pull off the skin. Remove the stems, seeds and ribs. Cut the peppers lengthwise into ½-inch strips.

**2.** In a large glass or stainless-steel bowl, using a fork, stir together the lemon juice, anchovy paste, vinegar, salt and pepper. Stir in the oil. Add the peppers and capers and toss.

**VARIATIONS**

🅥 Use halved and pitted **olives** in addition to or instead of the capers.
🅥 Add a sprinkling of chopped fresh **basil.**
🅥 Toss in a chopped **tomato.**
🅥 Use three chopped **anchovy fillets** instead of the paste.
🅥 Add a small can of drained **tuna.**

**SHORTCUT**

To roast the peppers quickly and with little mess, stand them upright and cut the flesh from each of the four sides, leaving the stem, seeds and core behind. Put the peppers on an aluminum-foil-lined baking sheet, cut-side down, and broil until charred. Peel off the blackened skin.

# fennel and red-onion salad with parmesan

*Crisp raw fennel, pungent onion and a sprightly lemon and orange dressing make for a delectable salad. A food processor with a slicing attachment cuts the fennel in no time.*

**PREP TIME**
10 MINUTES

**REST TIME**
5 MINUTES – 1 HOUR

**SERVES 4**

- 2 tablespoons lemon juice
- ¾ teaspoon grated orange zest
- 1½ tablespoons fresh orange juice
- ¾ teaspoon salt
- ¼ teaspoon fresh-ground black pepper
- 6 tablespoons olive oil
- 1¾ pounds fennel bulbs (about 2 large), cored and shaved as thin as possible
- 1 small red onion, chopped fine
- ½ cup grated Parmesan, or a chunk of Parmesan for making curls

**1.** In a large glass or stainless-steel bowl, whisk together the lemon juice, orange zest, orange juice, salt and ⅛ teaspoon of the pepper. Add the oil slowly, whisking. Add the fennel and onion and toss. Let stand at least 5 minutes but no more than 1 hour.

**2.** To serve, top the salad with the grated Parmesan, or with a few curls of Parmesan shaved from the chunk of cheese using a vegetable peeler. Sprinkle with the remaining ⅛ teaspoon pepper.

**VARIATION**

🅥 In addition to the orange zest and juice, add the **segments** from one **orange** to the salad.
*Using a stainless-steel knife, peel the orange down to the flesh, removing all of the white pith. Cut the sections away from the membranes. Squeeze the juice from the membranes to use in the dressing.*

**SLICING FENNEL BY HAND**

If you are slicing fennel by hand, the easiest way is to cut off the stalks, cut the bulb in half from the top through the root end, lay each half flat-side down and slice crosswise.

# grilled zucchini with fresh mozzarella

*The delicate taste of fresh mozzarella offers a delicious counterpoint to the garlic-and-vinegar-macerated zucchini. However, if you prefer a stronger cheese flavor, try goat cheese instead.*

**PREP TIME**
6 MINUTES

**COOK TIME**
10 MINUTES

**SERVES 4**

3 zucchini (about 1 pound), cut lengthwise into ¼-inch slices
2 tablespoons olive oil
Salt
Fresh-ground black pepper
¼ teaspoon wine vinegar
1 clove garlic, minced
1 tablespoon chopped flat-leaf parsley
½ pound salted fresh mozzarella, cut into thick slices

**1.** Light the grill or heat the broiler. In a large glass or stainless-steel bowl, toss the zucchini with 1 tablespoon of the oil, ¼ teaspoon salt and ⅛ teaspoon pepper. Grill or broil the zucchini, turning once, until tender and golden, about 5 minutes per side. Put the zucchini back in the bowl.

**2.** Toss the zucchini with ½ tablespoon of the oil, ⅛ teaspoon salt, the vinegar, garlic and parsley. Let cool.

**3.** Put the mozzarella slices on a serving plate, fanning them out to form a circle. Drizzle them with the remaining ½ tablespoon oil and sprinkle them with a pinch of pepper. Fold the zucchini slices in half and tuck them between the pieces of cheese.

### FRESH MOZZARELLA

Soft mozzarella is shaped into balls and stored in water to keep it moist. It is available both salted and unsalted, but the latter is very bland indeed. We prefer the salted variety; salting brings out the mild, milky flavor of the cheese.

# bruschetta duet

*We like the variety here—the same toast spread with two different toppings. The green-olive tapenade, which uses pre-pitted olives, can be made in minutes with a blender or food processor. The sautéed mushroom topping is equally savory hot or at room temperature.*

**PREP TIME**
10 MINUTES

**COOK TIME**
10 MINUTES

**SERVES 4**

- 8 tablespoons olive oil
- 2 teaspoons butter
- ¾ pound mushrooms, chopped fine
- 3 cloves garlic, 2 minced, 1 smashed
- ¼ teaspoon salt
- Fresh-ground black pepper
- ¼ teaspoon dried sage
- 1 tablespoon chopped flat-leaf parsley, plus ⅓ cup lightly packed leaves
- ½ cup pitted green olives
- ½ teaspoon anchovy paste
- 1½ teaspoons lemon juice
- Bruschetta, *opposite*

**1.** In a large frying pan, heat 2 tablespoons of the oil with the butter over moderately high heat. Add the mushrooms, the minced garlic, the salt, ⅛ teaspoon pepper and the sage. Cook, stirring occasionally, until the mushrooms are golden, 5 to 10 minutes. Stir in the chopped parsley. Remove from the heat.

**2.** In a blender or food processor, put the olives, parsley leaves, smashed garlic, anchovy paste, the remaining 6 tablespoons olive oil, the lemon juice and ¼ teaspoon pepper. Blend or process to a coarse puree.

**3.** Spread the mushroom mixture on eight of the bruschetta, and the tapenade on the rest.

**BRUSCHETTA**

**MAKES 16 BRUSCHETTA**

- 4 ½-inch-thick slices country bread
- 2 tablespoons olive oil
- ⅛ teaspoon salt

**1.** Heat the broiler. Put the bread on a baking sheet and brush both sides with the oil. Sprinkle with the salt.

**2.** Broil, turning once, until the bread is brown on the outside but still slightly soft in the center, about 3 minutes. Alternatively (and more traditionally), grill the bread. Cut each slice of bread into quarters.

# shrimp marinated in lemon and olive oil

*You'll want to gobble up these succulent morsels immediately, but patience will be rewarded; the shrimp taste better the longer they sit in the marinade. Leave them for a couple of hours, if you have the time.*

**PREP TIME**
6 MINUTES

**COOK TIME**
2 MINUTES

**SERVES 4**

- 1 **pound large shrimp, in their shells**
- 3½ **teaspoons lemon juice**
- 2 **tablespoons olive oil**
- 1 **tomato, seeded and cut into ¼-inch dice**
- ¼ **teaspoon salt**
- ⅛ **teaspoon fresh-ground black pepper**
- 2 **tablespoons chopped fresh parsley**

**1.** Bring a large pot of salted water to a boil. Add the shrimp, cover and bring back to a boil. Continue boiling, partially covered, until the shrimp are just done, 1 to 2 minutes. Drain. Let the shrimp cool and then peel them.

**2.** In a large glass or stainless-steel bowl, combine the lemon juice with the olive oil, tomato, salt, pepper and parsley. Add the shrimp and toss.

### VARIATIONS

**Ⓥ** Substitute a pound of **sea scallops** for the shrimp.
*Heat one tablespoon of oil in a large nonstick frying pan over moderately high heat until very hot. Season the scallops with one-eighth teaspoon salt. Put the scallops in the pan and sear until brown on the bottom, one to two minutes. Turn and brown on the other side until just done, one to two minutes longer. Remove the scallops and cut them into quarters. Toss with the marinade.*

**Ⓥ** Spice up the dish by adding one-quarter teaspoon dried **red-pepper flakes** to the marinade.

**Ⓥ** Use chopped fresh **basil** instead of the parsley.

**Ⓥ** For an extra flavor dimension, add a clove of minced **garlic** to the marinade.

# chopped italian salad

*Antipasto ingredients are sliced and diced to make a fun, flexible chopped salad. We've thrown in our favorites, and so should you. Add the dressing ingredients to the bowl, too, and mix them when you toss the salad—it's the Italian way.*

**PREP TIME**
15 MINUTES

**SERVES 4**

  1  head romaine lettuce (about 1¼ pounds), cut into 1-inch squares (about 3 quarts)
  ¼  pound sliced pepperoni, chopped
  ⅓  cup drained sliced pimientos (one 4-ounce jar)
  ⅓  cup chopped red onion
1½  cups drained, rinsed and chopped canned artichoke hearts (one 15-ounce can), or 1½ cups pitted and chopped green or black olives
  3  tablespoons red- or white-wine vinegar
  ¼  cup olive oil
  ½  teaspoon salt
  ¼  teaspoon fresh-ground black pepper
  ½  cup grated Parmesan

**1.** In a large glass or stainless-steel bowl, combine the romaine, pepperoni, pimientos, onion and the artichoke hearts or olives. Toss to combine.

**2.** Add the vinegar, oil, salt, pepper and Parmesan to the bowl. Toss thoroughly to combine the ingredients.

### VARIATIONS

Ⓥ Use chopped **salami** or **prosciutto** instead of the pepperoni.
Ⓥ Add some chopped **peperoncini** to spice up the salad.
Ⓥ Try a cup of drained and rinsed canned **chickpeas** instead of the artichoke hearts.
Ⓥ Diced **provolone cheese** would make a nice addition.
Ⓥ Stir in about a third of a cup of thin-sliced **basil** leaves.

# white-bean and prosciutto bruschetta

*Strips of prosciutto top each toast and are topped in turn with a mound of creamy white beans and a sprinkling of crisp red onion. If you like, serve these with the Bruschetta Duet on page 18 to make a tantalizing trio.*

**PREP TIME**
10 MINUTES

**SERVES 4**

2 cups drained and rinsed canned cannellini beans (one 19-ounce can)
1¼ teaspoons wine vinegar
1 tablespoon olive oil
¾ teaspoon chopped fresh thyme, or ¼ teaspoon dried thyme
¼ teaspoon salt
⅛ teaspoon fresh-ground black pepper
2½ tablespoons chopped fresh parsley
2 ounces thin-sliced prosciutto, fat removed, cut into thin strips
Bruschetta, *page 18*
2 tablespoons minced red onion

**1.** Put the beans in a medium glass or stainless-steel bowl. Using a fork, mash the beans to a coarse puree. Stir in the vinegar, oil, thyme, salt, pepper and 2 tablespoons of the parsley.

**2.** Put some of the prosciutto on each of the bruschetta and top with the bean mixture. Sprinkle the remaining ½ tablespoon parsley and the red onion over the beans.

**VARIATIONS**

Bruschetta can be topped with endless combinations of ingredients. Some of our favorites to try:
ⓥ Chopped **tomato** and **basil**
ⓥ Diced **roasted bell peppers** with crumbled **goat cheese**
ⓥ Drained canned **tuna** and **capers**
ⓥ Strips of **Parmigiano-Reggiano**
ⓥ A split **garlic** clove rubbed over the toast, followed by a generous drizzle of **olive oil**

RISI E BISI WITH HAM AND PARMESAN, P. 38

# 2

# *soups*

# chickpea soup with swiss chard

*The humble chickpea is enormously popular in Italy, especially for soups. Here, in this Tuscan specialty, it's joined by tomatoes, macaroni, Swiss-chard leaves and a generous quantity of garlic.*

**PREP TIME**
10 MINUTES

**COOK TIME**
25 MINUTES

**SERVES 4**

6   cups drained and rinsed canned chickpeas (three 19-ounce cans)
3   cups canned low-sodium chicken broth or homemade stock, more if needed
3   tablespoons olive oil
1   carrot, chopped
1   onion, chopped
1   rib celery, chopped
4   cloves garlic, minced
1   teaspoon dried rosemary, or 1 tablespoon chopped fresh rosemary
1   bay leaf
Pinch dried red-pepper flakes
1   cup canned tomatoes in thick puree, chopped
½   cup tubetti or other small macaroni
1   teaspoon salt
½   pound Swiss chard, tough stems removed, leaves cut into 1-inch pieces
¼   teaspoon fresh-ground black pepper

**1.** Puree half of the chickpeas with 1½ cups of the broth in a blender or food processor. In a large pot, heat the oil over moderately low heat. Add the carrot, onion, celery, garlic and rosemary and cook, stirring occasionally, until the vegetables start to soften, about 5 minutes.

**2.** Stir in the remaining 1½ cups broth, the pureed chickpeas, whole chickpeas, bay leaf, red-pepper flakes, tomatoes, tubetti and salt. Bring to a boil. Reduce the heat and simmer, partially covered, for 10 minutes.

**3.** Add the Swiss chard to the pot. Simmer until the chard is tender and the pasta is done, 5 to 10 minutes longer. Remove the bay leaf. Stir in the black pepper. If the soup thickens too much on standing, stir in more broth or water.

## wine recommendation

Since a red wine would accent the Swiss chard's bitterness, try a full-bodied tocai friulano. Its nutty flavor will mirror that of the chickpeas.

# minestrone with arborio rice

*There are as many versions of minestrone as there are cooks in Italy, but the soup always contains a variety of vegetables and usually includes beans and either pasta or rice. If you happen to have a Parmigiano-Reggiano rind on hand, throw that into the soup pot as well. If the minestrone becomes too thick, simply thin it with water or add more stock.*

**PREP TIME**
10 MINUTES

**COOK TIME**
40 MINUTES

**SERVES 4**

¼ cup plus 4 teaspoons olive oil
1 onion, chopped
2 cloves garlic, minced
2 carrots, cut into ¼-inch dice
2 ribs celery, sliced
1 zucchini, cut in quarters lengthwise and then crosswise into thin slices
¾ pound green cabbage (about ¼ head), shredded (about 3 cups)
1½ quarts canned low-sodium chicken broth or homemade stock
1⅔ cups drained and rinsed canned pinto beans (one 15-ounce can)
½ cup arborio rice
¾ pound boiling potatoes (about 2), peeled and cut into ¼-inch dice
1 tablespoon tomato paste
1 bay leaf
½ teaspoon dried thyme
2¼ teaspoons salt
¼ teaspoon fresh-ground black pepper
2 tablespoons grated Parmesan

**1.** In a large pot, heat the ¼ cup oil over moderate heat. Add the onion and cook, stirring occasionally, until golden, about 10 minutes. Add the garlic, carrots and celery. Cook, stirring occasionally, for 5 minutes. Add the zucchini and cabbage. Cook, stirring occasionally, until the vegetables start to soften, about 5 minutes longer.

**2.** Add the broth, beans, rice, potatoes, tomato paste, bay leaf, thyme and salt to the pot. Bring to a boil. Reduce the heat and simmer, partially covered, until the rice and vegetables are tender, about 15 minutes. Remove the bay leaf.

**3.** Stir the pepper into the soup. Sprinkle each bowlful with Parmesan and drizzle each with 1 teaspoon of the remaining oil.

## wine recommendation

Salice Salentino, a rich and rustic red from southern Italy's Apulia, is a heartwarming match for this familiar classic. The wine is produced in vast quantities, making it a snap to find.

# split-pea soup with portobellos

*Meaty portobellos are especially good for adding substance and flavor to this soup, but shiitake or other mushrooms will work well, too. You can also add a ham hock to the pot while the split peas cook, if you like.*

**PREP TIME**
8 MINUTES

**COOK TIME**
50 MINUTES

**SERVES 4**

4 tablespoons olive oil
2 carrots, chopped
2 onions, chopped
2 ribs celery, chopped
3 cloves garlic, minced
1⅔ cups green split peas
3 tablespoons chopped fresh parsley
9 cups water
½ teaspoon dried thyme
1 bay leaf
2 teaspoons salt
1 pound portobello mushrooms, stems removed, caps cut into ½-inch dice
6 tablespoons grated Parmesan
¼ teaspoon fresh-ground black pepper

**1.** In a large pot, heat 2 tablespoons of the oil over moderate heat. Add the carrots, onions, celery and garlic. Cook, stirring occasionally, until the vegetables start to soften, about 5 minutes.

**2.** Add the split peas, parsley, water, thyme and bay leaf. Bring to a boil. Reduce the heat and cook at a low boil, covered, until the peas are almost tender, about 35 minutes. Add 1¾ teaspoons of the salt and simmer 5 minutes longer. Remove the bay leaf.

**3.** Meanwhile, in a large nonstick frying pan, heat the remaining 2 tablespoons oil over moderately high heat. Add the mushrooms and the remaining ¼ teaspoon salt. Cook until the mushrooms brown, 5 to 10 minutes. Add the mushrooms to the soup and bring back to a simmer. Stir in the Parmesan and pepper.

## wine recommendation

You'll need a white wine with body and lots of character to stand up to a hearty pea soup like this one. Greco di Tufo, with its full texture and big, nutty taste, is made for the job.

# venetian fish soup

*You can, and should, make this with whatever firm or moderately firm fish looks best in the market. For a delicious traditional addition to the soup, toast four slices of good country-style bread and rub each piece with the cut-side of a halved garlic clove. Put a piece of toast in the bottom of each bowl and ladle the soup over it.*

**PREP TIME**
15 MINUTES

**COOK TIME**
50 MINUTES

**SERVES 4**

½ pound large shrimp, shells removed and reserved
2 cups water
3 tablespoons olive oil
2 carrots, chopped
2 onions, chopped
1 fennel bulb, chopped
2 ribs celery, chopped
6 cloves garlic, minced
½ cup dry white wine
3½ cups bottled clam juice
2½ cups canned crushed tomatoes in thick puree (from a 28-ounce can)
¼ teaspoon dried red-pepper flakes
5 tablespoons chopped fresh parsley
½ teaspoon dried thyme
1 teaspoon salt or more, depending on the saltiness of the clam juice
2 bay leaves
2 pounds moderately firm white fish fillets (use 2 or 3 types), such as cod, halibut, red snapper or tilapia, cut into 1-inch chunks
⅛ teaspoon fresh-ground black pepper

**1.** Put the shrimp shells and the water in a small pot; bring the water to a boil. Reduce the heat and simmer, covered, for 15 minutes. Strain the shrimp stock into a bowl. Discard the shells.

**2.** In a large pot, heat the oil over moderate heat. Add the carrots, onions, fennel, celery and garlic; cook, stirring occasionally, until the vegetables start to soften, about 5 minutes. Add the wine; cook until it almost evaporates, about 5 minutes. Stir in the shrimp stock, clam juice, tomatoes, red-pepper flakes, 4 tablespoons of the parsley, the thyme, salt and bay leaves. Bring to a boil. Reduce the heat and simmer, partially covered, for 25 minutes. Taste for salt and, if needed, add more. Remove the bay leaves.

**3.** Add the fish, shrimp, the remaining 1 tablespoon parsley and the pepper to the pot and bring to a simmer. Simmer until the fish and shrimp are just done, about 2 minutes.

## wine recommendation

Tomato-based fish dishes are just fine with red wine. Here, a refreshingly light and fruity Bardolino from the Veneto will be perfect.

# minestrone with sole

*Thick and chunky with vegetables and pieces of sole, this pesto-flavored soup is hearty enough to make a meal. Serve it hot to take the chill off a winter night, or at room temperature for a cool summertime supper.*

**PREP TIME**
10 MINUTES

**COOK TIME**
40 MINUTES

**SERVES 4**

 1 tablespoon butter
 3 tablespoons olive oil
 1 onion, chopped
 2 cloves garlic, minced
 2 carrots, cut into ¼-inch dice
 2 ribs celery, cut into ¼-inch dice
 ¾ pound boiling potatoes (about 2), peeled and cut into ¼-inch dice
 1 zucchini, cut into ¼-inch dice
 ¼ head cabbage (about ¾ pound), shredded
3¾ cups canned low-sodium chicken broth or homemade stock
1½ cups drained and rinsed canned pinto beans (one 15-ounce can)
 1 tablespoon tomato paste
1½ teaspoons salt
1½ pounds sole fillets, cut into 1-inch pieces
 2 tablespoons pesto, store-bought or homemade
 ¼ teaspoon fresh-ground black pepper

**1.** In a large pot, melt the butter with the oil over moderate heat. Add the onion and cook, stirring occasionally, until golden, about 5 minutes. Add the garlic, carrots, celery and potatoes and cook, stirring occasionally, for 5 minutes. Add the zucchini and cabbage and cook, stirring occasionally, for 5 minutes longer.

**2.** Add the broth, beans, tomato paste and salt and bring to a simmer. Simmer, partially covered, until the vegetables are tender, about 18 minutes. Add the sole, pesto and pepper and bring back to a simmer. Cook, uncovered, until the fish is just done, about 1 to 2 minutes more. To serve, ladle into bowls and pass more pesto if you like.

**VARIATIONS**

**V** You can use any other member of the flounder family, such as **sand dab** or **fluke,** in place of the sole. Or try a firmer white fish, such as **cod, halibut** or **monkfish.** For these thicker fish, add another minute to the cooking time.

## wine recommendation

A light Italian white wine will be delightful with the vegetables and pesto. Look for the most recent vintage of a pinot grigio from the northern Alto Adige region.

# risi e bisi with ham and parmesan

*A favorite of the rice-loving Venetians, the soup called* risi e bisi *(rice and peas) is so thick that it's sometimes mistaken for risotto. We've added diced ham and plenty of Parmesan to make a satisfying dinner.*

**PREP TIME**
15 MINUTES

**COOK TIME**
45 MINUTES

**SERVES 4**

- 6 tablespoons butter
- 1 onion, chopped
- 1 rib celery, chopped
- 1 large clove garlic, minced
- ½ cup dry white wine
- 2 quarts canned low-sodium chicken broth or homemade stock
- 1½ cups rice, preferably arborio
- 2 tablespoons chopped fresh parsley
- 1¾ teaspoons salt
- 2 cups frozen petite peas (one 10-ounce package), defrosted
- 1 ¼-pound piece deli ham, cut into small dice
- ¾ cup grated Parmesan
- ½ teaspoon fresh-ground black pepper

**1.** In a large pot, melt the butter over moderately low heat. Add the onion, celery and garlic and cook, stirring occasionally, until the vegetables start to soften, about 5 minutes. Add the wine and boil until it almost evaporates, about 5 minutes. Add the broth and bring to a boil. Boil until the liquid is reduced to approximately 7 cups, about 20 minutes.

**2.** Add the rice, parsley and salt and cook at a low boil, stirring occasionally, until the rice is just tender, 10 to 15 minutes. Stir in the peas, ham, Parmesan and pepper.

**PETITE PEAS**

Peas are one of the few vegetables that are usually better frozen than fresh. Frozen petite peas consistently have good flavor, a pleasant sweetness and tender texture. In the springtime, if you can find truly fresh, sweet peas, by all means use them here. Just add them with the rice and parsley.

## wine recommendation

A light and unpretentious red will make the best partner for this dish. Look to the Veneto for the tart-cherry flavor of a crisp Bardolino or a slightly fuller Valpolicella.

# lentil soup with tubetti and bacon

*Vegetables, lentils and pasta simmer in a broth. The soup is infused with the earthy flavors of bacon and rosemary. We use tubetti, but any small macaroni shape will work as well.*

**PREP TIME**
10 MINUTES

**COOK TIME**
40 MINUTES

**SERVES 4**

¼ pound bacon, slices cut crosswise into ½-inch strips
2 carrots, cut into 1-inch pieces
2 onions, cut into 1-inch chunks
2 ribs celery, cut into 1-inch pieces
½ pound mushrooms, sliced
6 cloves garlic, sliced
1 pound lentils (about 2⅓ cups)
1½ quarts canned low-sodium chicken broth or homemade stock
3 cups water
1 teaspoon dried rosemary, or 1 tablespoon chopped fresh rosemary
1 cup canned tomatoes in thick puree, chopped
2 teaspoons salt
¼ teaspoon dried red-pepper flakes
¼ teaspoon fresh-ground black pepper
½ cup tubetti or other small macaroni

**1.** In a large pot, cook the bacon over moderate heat until crisp. Remove. Pour off all but 2 tablespoons of the fat. Add the carrots, onions, celery, mushrooms and garlic. Cook, stirring occasionally, until the vegetables start to soften, about 5 minutes.

**2.** Add the lentils, broth, water, rosemary, tomatoes, salt, red-pepper flakes, black pepper and bacon. Bring to a boil. Reduce the heat and simmer for 15 minutes. Add the pasta and simmer until the lentils are tender and the pasta is done, 10 to 15 minutes longer.

**VARIATIONS**

Ⓥ Substitute an equal amount of **pancetta** for the bacon.
Ⓥ Use **thyme** instead of rosemary.
Ⓥ Add shredded **spinach** or **escarole** leaves during the last few minutes of cooking.

## wine recommendation

The nebbiolo grape produces wine with complex notes including smoke, truffle and dried red cherry. A light-bodied version, such as one from Valtellina, is an excellent match.

# pasta e fagioli with sausage

*The much-beloved* pasta e fagioli *(pasta and beans), adorned here with sliced sausage, is truly a meal in itself. The soup has very little liquid and will thicken as it sits. If you'd like to thin it a bit, add a little more chicken broth or water.*

**PREP TIME**
10 MINUTES

**COOK TIME**
50 MINUTES

**SERVES 4**

2  tablespoons olive oil
1  pound mild Italian sausages
1  carrot, chopped fine
1  onion, chopped fine
1  rib celery, chopped fine
4  cloves garlic, minced
1  teaspoon dried rosemary, or 1 tablespoon chopped fresh rosemary
6  cups drained and rinsed canned kidney beans (three 19-ounce cans)
2¾  cups canned low-sodium chicken broth or homemade stock
1  bay leaf
1  teaspoon salt
½  cup tubetti or other small macaroni
½  teaspoon fresh-ground black pepper

**1.** In a large pot, heat 1 tablespoon of the oil over moderate heat. Add the sausages and cook, turning, until browned and cooked through, about 10 minutes. Remove. When cool enough to handle, halve the sausages lengthwise and then cut crosswise into slices.

**2.** Heat the remaining 1 tablespoon oil in the pot over moderately low heat. Add the carrot, onion, celery, garlic and rosemary. Cook, stirring occasionally, until the vegetables start to soften, about 10 minutes.

**3.** Puree 4 cups of the beans with 1¼ cups of the broth in a blender or food processor. Add the puree to the pot along with the remaining 1½ cups broth, the whole beans, bay leaf and salt. Bring to a boil. Reduce the heat and simmer, partially covered, for 15 minutes.

**4.** Stir in the pasta. Cook the soup over moderate heat, partially covered, stirring frequently, until the pasta is done, 10 to 15 minutes. Remove the bay leaf. Stir in the sausage and the pepper. Cook until the sausage is warmed through, about 1 minute.

## wine recommendation

This hearty favorite is best accompanied by a light, sprightly grignolino. Almost more rosé than red wine, grignolino has a penetrating floral aroma and spicy flavor.

# sausage and mushroom soup

*Strands of angel-hair pasta form a web in the broth, capturing the slices of sausage and mushroom. Red-pepper flakes give the soup its spiciness; to turn up the heat another notch, use hot Italian sausage instead of mild.*

**PREP TIME**
6 MINUTES

**COOK TIME**
40 MINUTES

**SERVES 4**

- 2 tablespoons olive oil
- 1¼ pounds mild Italian sausages
- 1 onion, chopped
- 3 cloves garlic, minced
- 1 pound mushrooms, sliced
- 7 cups canned low-sodium chicken broth or homemade stock
- ½ teaspoon dried thyme
- ¼ teaspoon dried red-pepper flakes
- 4 tablespoons chopped fresh parsley
- 1¾ teaspoons salt
- ¼ pound angel hair
- ⅛ teaspoon fresh-ground black pepper

**1.** In a large pot, heat 1 tablespoon of the oil over moderate heat. Add the sausages and cook, turning occasionally, until browned and cooked through, about 10 minutes. Remove. When cool enough to handle, cut the sausages into ⅛-inch slices.

**2.** Heat the remaining 1 tablespoon oil in the pot over moderately low heat. Add the onion and garlic and cook, stirring occasionally, until the onion is translucent, about 5 minutes. Add the mushrooms and cook until golden, 5 to 10 minutes.

**3.** Add the broth, thyme, red-pepper flakes, 2 tablespoons of the parsley and the salt to the pot. Bring to a boil. Reduce the heat and simmer, partially covered, for 15 minutes. Stir in the sausage and bring back to a boil. Add the pasta, reduce the heat and simmer until just done, about 3 minutes. Stir in the remaining 2 tablespoons parsley and the black pepper.

## wine recommendation

A Valtellina from northern Piedmont will nicely echo the earthy mushroom and spicy sausage flavors here. The wine is made from the nebbiolo grape, as are the more familiar Barolo and Barbaresco.

# sicilian meatball soup

*Flavored with Parmesan and garlic and studded with raisins, scrumptious Sicilian meatballs turn vegetable soup into a tempting meal. If the soup waits, the pasta may absorb much of the liquid; just add water or more stock.*

**PREP TIME**
10 MINUTES

**COOK TIME**
30 MINUTES

**SERVES 4**

- ½ **pound ground beef**
- 5 **tablespoons chopped fresh parsley**
- ¼ **cup grated Parmesan, plus more for serving**
- 2 **tablespoons raisins**
- 2 **tablespoons dry bread crumbs**
- 1 **egg, beaten**
- 5 **cloves garlic, minced**
- 2½ **teaspoons salt**
- ½ **teaspoon fresh-ground black pepper**
- 2 **tablespoons olive oil**
- 2 **carrots, cut into ¼-inch dice**
- 1 **onion, chopped**
- 2 **ribs celery, cut into ¼-inch dice**
- 1 **zucchini, cut into ¼-inch dice**
- 1½ **quarts canned low-sodium chicken broth or homemade stock**
- 1 **cup canned crushed tomatoes in thick puree**
- ½ **teaspoon dried rosemary, or 2 teaspoons chopped fresh rosemary**
- 1 **cup small pasta shells or other small macaroni**

**1.** In a medium bowl, mix together the ground beef, 4 tablespoons of the parsley, the Parmesan, raisins, bread crumbs, egg, half of the garlic, ½ teaspoon of the salt and ¼ teaspoon of the pepper until thoroughly combined. Shape the mixture into 24 meatballs.

**2.** In a large pot, heat the oil over moderate heat. Add the carrots, onion, celery and the remaining garlic and cook, stirring occasionally, until the vegetables start to soften, about 5 minutes. Add the zucchini and cook, stirring occasionally, for 5 minutes. Stir in the broth, tomatoes, rosemary and the remaining 2 teaspoons salt. Bring to a boil. Reduce the heat and simmer, partially covered, for 10 minutes.

**3.** Add the remaining 1 tablespoon parsley, ¼ teaspoon pepper and the pasta to the soup. Simmer for 5 minutes. Stir in the meatballs and simmer gently until the meatballs and pasta are done, about 5 minutes longer. Serve with additional Parmesan.

## wine recommendation

This robust potion calls for a similarly rustic southern red. Look for Corvo, a smooth and satisfying wine from the well-known firm Duca di Salaparuta.

RIGATONI WITH SAUSAGE AND
TOMATO CREAM SAUCE, P. 76

# 3

# *pasta*

# fusilli with zucchini and fonduta

*The classic Piedmontese* fonduta *combines fontina cheese, milk, egg yolks and butter into a silky sauce that's usually topped with thin slices of white truffle. Traditionally,* fonduta *is served with toast or fried polenta. Our version (minus the truffle) coats fusilli and strips of zucchini for a divine rendition of macaroni and cheese.*

**PREP TIME**
8 MINUTES

**COOK TIME**
15 MINUTES

**REST TIME**
20 MINUTES

**SERVES 4**

¾  pound fontina, grated (about 3 cups)
1¼  cups milk
3  egg yolks
3  tablespoons butter, cut into pieces, at room temperature
1¼  teaspoons salt
½  teaspoon fresh-ground black pepper
1  pound fusilli
4  zucchini (about 1½ pounds), seeded and cut into ¼-by-2-inch matchstick strips

**1.** In a medium heatproof bowl, combine the grated cheese and the milk. Allow the mixture to stand for 20 minutes and then drain off the milk, reserving ¼ cup. Set the bowl with the cheese over a saucepan of barely simmering water, or transfer the cheese to the top of a double boiler. Whisk until the cheese melts, about 5 minutes.

**2.** In a small bowl, whisk together the egg yolks and the reserved ¼ cup milk and add to the melted cheese with the butter, whisking. The mixture will separate. Add the salt and pepper and continue whisking until the sauce is almost smooth, about 3 minutes longer. Do not cook too long or the mixture will curdle. The sauce will not be completely smooth.

**3.** Meanwhile, in a large pot of boiling, salted water, cook the fusilli for 10 minutes. Add the zucchini and bring back to a boil. Cook until the zucchini and pasta are just done, about 3 minutes longer. Drain. Toss with the *fonduta*.

### SEEDING ZUCCHINI

Because the zucchini are boiled here, we recommend seeding them first; otherwise, the pulpy seeds become waterlogged. To remove the seeds, cut the zucchini into quarters lengthwise. Then simply cut off the seeds.

## wine recommendation

Do not try to match this dish's richness; go for contrast instead. Piedmont's own Nebbiolo delle Langhe, a spicy, earthy red wine with subtle hints of truffle, is what you want.

# spaghetti with tomatoes, basil, olives and fresh mozzarella

*Since the tomatoes here are not cooked, you'll really notice their flavor—or lack of it. Make this sauce in the summer when fresh tomatoes are at their peak. The garlic is heated briefly in the oil, and then the garlicky oil is tossed with the spaghetti so the flavor is dispersed throughout the dish. The pasta is equally good warm and at room temperature.*

**PREP TIME**
8 MINUTES

**COOK TIME**
15 MINUTES

**SERVES 4**

2 pounds vine-ripened tomatoes (about 6), chopped
¾ pound salted fresh mozzarella, cut into ¼-inch cubes, at room temperature
1¼ cups chopped fresh basil
½ cup halved and pitted black olives
4 teaspoons balsamic vinegar
1¼ teaspoons salt
½ teaspoon fresh-ground black pepper
1 pound spaghetti
½ cup olive oil
3 cloves garlic, minced

**1.** In a large glass or stainless-steel bowl, combine the chopped tomatoes with the mozzarella, basil, olives, balsamic vinegar, salt and pepper.

**2.** In a large pot of boiling, salted water, cook the spaghetti until just done, about 12 minutes. Drain, add to the tomato mixture and toss.

**3.** Heat the oil in a small frying pan over moderately low heat. Add the garlic and cook, stirring, for 1 minute. Pour the oil over the pasta and toss again.

**VARIATIONS**

Ⓥ Add some drained **capers**, chopped **red onion** or grated **Parmesan** to the pasta.

wine recommendation

Valpolicella, the crisp, fruity, cherry-scented wine from the shores of Lake Garda in the Veneto, is the perfect hot-weather wine for tomato-and-herb-based dishes. Try one here for a delightful accompaniment.

# ziti, eggplant and fontina gratin

*Eggplant is sautéed in olive oil until it's creamy soft and then tossed with pasta and cheese. A quick stint under the broiler melts the fontina and browns the top.*

**PREP TIME**
10 MINUTES

**COOK TIME**
30 MINUTES

**SERVES 4**

- 7 tablespoons olive oil
- 1 large eggplant (about 1¾ pounds), peeled and cut into ¼-inch dice
- 1¼ teaspoons salt
- 2 cloves garlic, minced
- 3 tablespoons chopped fresh parsley
- ½ teaspoon fresh-ground black pepper
- 1 pound ziti or penne
- ½ pound fontina, grated (about 2 cups)

**1.** In a large nonstick frying pan, heat 4 tablespoons of the oil over moderately high heat. Add the eggplant and ¾ teaspoon of the salt and cook, stirring frequently, until the eggplant is soft, 10 to 15 minutes. Stir in the garlic, parsley and ¼ teaspoon of the pepper and cook 3 minutes longer.

**2.** Heat the broiler. In a large pot of boiling, salted water, cook the pasta until just done, about 10 to 15 minutes. Drain.

**3.** Toss the pasta with the eggplant, the remaining 3 tablespoons oil, ½ teaspoon salt and ¼ teaspoon pepper. Add the cheese and toss again. Transfer the pasta to a shallow baking dish or gratin dish. Broil until the cheese melts and starts to brown, 2 to 3 minutes.

## EGGPLANT CONTROVERSIES

Cooks in Italy, as everywhere, disagree about whether or not eggplant should be peeled. It seems to be a matter of personal preference, but keep in mind that an eggplant that is overgrown or has been stored for a long time will have a tough skin that will not soften during cooking. It's often a good idea to peel it.

Whether or not to salt and drain eggplant before cooking remains a matter of dispute, too. Some say you should salt slices heavily and drain them on paper towels for an hour to rid the eggplant of any bitterness; others feel it's an unnecessary step. What is indisputably true is that eggplant that has been salted and drained will absorb less oil during frying than eggplant that has not.

## wine recommendation

Though *dolcetto* translates as "little sweet one," that refers to the grape; the wine is delightfully dry. It will make an ideal partner for this tasty dish.

# linguine with cauliflower, garlic and bread crumbs

*The strong flavors of cauliflower, garlic, red-pepper flakes and Parmesan cheese balance perfectly, raising these common, readily available ingredients to new heights.*

**PREP TIME**
10 MINUTES

**COOK TIME**
15 MINUTES

**SERVES 4**

- 8 tablespoons olive oil
- 1 cup fresh bread crumbs
- 6 cloves garlic, minced
- 6 tablespoons chopped fresh parsley
- ½ teaspoon dried red-pepper flakes
- 1 teaspoon anchovy paste
- 1 pound linguine
- 1 head cauliflower (about 2½ pounds), cut into small florets
- 1 teaspoon salt
- ½ cup grated Parmesan, plus more for serving

**1.** In a large frying pan, heat 4 tablespoons of the oil over moderate heat. Add the bread crumbs and cook, stirring, until golden, about 5 minutes. Remove. Wipe out the pan.

**2.** Heat the remaining 4 tablespoons oil in the same pan over moderately low heat. Add the garlic, parsley and red-pepper flakes. Cook, stirring, for 1 minute. Stir in the anchovy paste. Remove from the heat.

**3.** In a large pot of boiling, salted water, cook the linguine until almost done, about 8 minutes. Add the cauliflower and bring back to a boil. Cook until the cauliflower and pasta are just done, about 4 minutes longer. Drain. Toss with the garlic mixture, salt, bread crumbs and Parmesan. Top with additional Parmesan.

**VARIATIONS**

- Ⓥ Substitute **broccoli** for the cauliflower.
- Ⓥ Add a handful each of **raisins** and **pine nuts** at the same time as the garlic, parsley and red-pepper flakes.
- Ⓥ Use four chopped **anchovy fillets** instead of the anchovy paste.

## wine recommendation

Red wine, if it's simple and crisp, makes an intriguing choice for this dish. A touch of earthiness, such as you'll find in a basic Chianti, helps to tie the wine and food flavors together.

# baked rigatoni with spinach, ricotta and fontina

*A quick take on spinach and ricotta cannelloni, this baked pasta is fast because there's nothing to stuff. The filling is simply tossed with cooked rigatoni that's then topped with fontina and baked to a golden brown.*

**PREP TIME**
5 MINUTES

**COOK TIME**
30 MINUTES

**SERVES 4**

- 1 pound rigatoni
- 3 tablespoons olive oil
- 1 10-ounce package frozen spinach, thawed
- 2 cups (about 1 pound) ricotta
- 5 tablespoons grated Parmesan
- ½ teaspoon grated nutmeg
- ¾ teaspoon salt
- ¼ teaspoon fresh-ground black pepper
- 6 ounces fontina, grated (about 1½ cups)

**1.** Heat the oven to 450°. Oil a 9-by-13-inch baking dish.

**2.** In a large pot of boiling, salted water, cook the rigatoni until almost done, about 12 minutes. Drain. Put the pasta in the prepared baking dish and toss with 1 tablespoon of the oil.

**3.** Meanwhile, squeeze as much of the water as possible from the spinach. Put the spinach in a food processor and puree with the ricotta, 3 tablespoons of the Parmesan, the nutmeg, salt and pepper. Stir in half the fontina.

**4.** Stir the spinach mixture into the pasta. Top with the remaining fontina and Parmesan. Drizzle the remaining 2 tablespoons oil over the top. Bake the pasta until the top is golden brown, 15 to 20 minutes.

**VARIATION**

ⓥ You can substitute another chunky pasta, such as **penne rigate, penne, ziti** or **fusilli.** Boil all of these one or two minutes less.

## wine recommendation

A delicately flavored white such as Orvieto will complement the mild ricotta nicely. And because Orvieto is not oaky, the wine has no bitter tannin to clash with the slightly bitter spinach and nutmeg.

# fettuccine alfredo with asparagus

*Ready to go at a moment's notice, this asparagus-embellished classic is not only creamy, quick and delicious, but it dirties only one pot.*

**PREP TIME**
5 MINUTES

**COOK TIME**
12 MINUTES

**SERVES 4**

1 pound asparagus
¾ pound fettuccine
4 tablespoons butter, cut into pieces
1 cup heavy cream
Pinch grated nutmeg
¾ teaspoon salt
⅛ teaspoon fresh-ground black pepper
½ cup grated Parmesan, plus more for serving

**1.** Snap the tough ends off the asparagus and discard them. Cut the asparagus spears into 1-inch pieces. In a large pot of boiling, salted water, cook the fettuccine until almost done, about 8 minutes. Add the asparagus; cook until it and the pasta are just done, about 4 minutes longer.

**2.** Drain the pasta and asparagus. Toss with the butter, cream, nutmeg, salt, pepper and Parmesan. Serve with additional Parmesan.

**VARIATIONS**

**Ⓥ Fettuccine Alfredo**
*Eliminate the asparagus.*

**Ⓥ Fettuccine Alfredo with Ham and Peas**
*Eliminate the asparagus. Add one cup frozen peas to the pasta during the last two minutes of cooking. Toss a quarter pound deli ham, cut into matchstick strips, with the remaining ingredients.*

**Ⓥ Fettuccine Alfredo with Fresh Mixed Herbs**
*Eliminate the asparagus. Toss in three tablespoons chopped fresh herbs, such as basil, parsley and/or chives, at the end.*

**Ⓥ Fettuccine Alfredo with Parsley and Sage**
*Eliminate the asparagus. Toss in two tablespoons chopped fresh parsley and a half teaspoon dried sage at the end.*

## wine recommendation

A forcefully acidic white wine is a natural with asparagus and will pierce the richness of the sauce. Try one of the sauvignon blancs from New Zealand or a vernaccia from Italy.

# penne arrabbiata with flaked cod

*Arrabbiata means "angry" and is often used to describe a spicy tomato sauce. Cook the cod directly in the sauce and then break it into flakes. If you prefer, you can use another fish with large flakes, such as orange roughy or haddock, instead of the cod.*

PREP TIME
7 MINUTES

COOK TIME
30 MINUTES

**SERVES 4**

¼  cup olive oil
2  cloves garlic, minced
3  cups canned crushed tomatoes in thick puree (one 28-ounce can)
1  large tomato, peeled and chopped
1¾  teaspoons salt
½  teaspoon dried red-pepper flakes
1  pound cod fillet, cut into 1-inch chunks
3  tablespoons chopped fresh parsley
1  pound penne

**1.** In a large saucepan, heat the oil over moderate heat. Add the garlic and cook, stirring, for 1 minute. Add the canned tomatoes, fresh tomato, salt and red-pepper flakes and bring to a simmer. Simmer the sauce until thick, about 30 minutes.

**2.** Add the cod and 2 tablespoons of the parsley to the sauce. Bring back to a simmer and continue simmering until the fish is just done, 1 to 2 minutes. Break the fish into small pieces with a spoon.

**3.** Meanwhile, in a large pot of boiling, salted water, cook the penne until just done, about 13 minutes. Drain. Toss with the sauce. Top the pasta with the remaining 1 tablespoon parsley.

### VARIATION

Ⓥ To make this dish without a trip to the fish market, substitute two six-ounce cans of drained **tuna** for the cod. *Stir it into the tomato sauce and warm for about a minute before tossing with the pasta.*

### TEST-KITCHEN TIP

To peel the fresh tomato quickly, make double use of the pasta-cooking water. Bring a pot of water to a boil, core the tomato and drop it into the water for fifteen seconds. Using a slotted spoon, remove the tomato from the water, peel and chop it. Then you've got boiling water ready for the pasta.

## wine recommendation

The adage is white wine with fish, but the tomatoes in this sauce call for a red instead. Try a sprightly Lago di Caldero or an easier-to-find Valpolicella.

# linguine with tuna, walnuts, lemon and herbs

*Keep tuna on hand for quick, last-minute pasta sauces. Lemon zest, lemon juice and tons of fresh herbs brighten this one. Though Italian cooks stick to canned tuna for this kind of sauce, you might try it with fresh tuna steaks, seared and sliced.*

**PREP TIME**
10 MINUTES

**COOK TIME**
15 MINUTES

**SERVES 4**

¾  cup walnuts, chopped
1  pound linguine
⅓  cup olive oil
4  cloves garlic, minced
2  6-ounce cans tuna packed in oil
2  teaspoons grated lemon zest (from 2 lemons)
2  teaspoons lemon juice
¾  teaspoon salt
½  teaspoon fresh-ground black pepper
½  cup mixed chopped fresh herbs, such as parsley, chives and thyme

**1.** In a small frying pan, toast the walnuts over moderately low heat, stirring frequently, until golden brown, about 5 minutes. Or toast them in a 350° oven for 5 to 10 minutes.

**2.** In a large pot of boiling, salted water, cook the linguine until just done, about 12 minutes. Drain.

**3.** Meanwhile, in a large frying pan, heat the olive oil over moderate heat. Add the garlic and cook, stirring, for 1 minute. Stir in the tuna and its oil and break up the tuna with a fork. Remove from the heat. Toss the linguine with the tuna mixture, the lemon zest, lemon juice, salt, pepper, herbs and the toasted walnuts.

**CANNED TUNA**

Brands of tuna vary tremendously. Here we use tuna packed in oil (preferably olive oil), and we count on that oil as part of the sauce. If your tuna has less than one and a half tablespoons oil per can, add more olive oil to make up the difference.

## wine recommendation

Wines of Italy's Alto Adige show a strong Germanic influence due to the region's proximity to Switzerland. Try a flowery, lime-scented Müller-Thurgau for a refreshing change from the ordinary.

# spaghetti with squid in tomato wine sauce

*Inexpensive and easy to prepare, squid deserves a place in your weeknight repertoire. Here, it's gently simmered in a garlicky red-wine tomato sauce and then tossed with pasta for a meal that's quick to put together.*

**PREP TIME**
6 MINUTES

**COOK TIME**
35 MINUTES

**SERVES 4**

| | |
|---|---|
| 1 | tablespoon cooking oil |
| 3 | cloves garlic, minced |
| ⅓ | cup red wine |
| 1¾ | cups canned crushed tomatoes in thick puree |
| ¾ | teaspoon salt |
| 1 | pound cleaned squid, bodies cut into ½-inch rings, tentacles cut in half |
| ½ | pound spaghetti |
| ⅓ | cup chopped fresh basil or parsley |

**1.** In a large saucepan, heat the oil over moderately low heat. Add the garlic and cook, stirring, for 1 minute. Add the wine and simmer 1 minute longer. Stir in the tomatoes and salt and bring to a simmer. Add the squid, cover and simmer gently until the squid is just tender, about 30 minutes. Do not allow to boil.

**2.** Meanwhile, in a large pot of boiling, salted water, cook the spaghetti until almost done, about 10 minutes. Drain the pasta.

**3.** Add the basil and spaghetti to the sauce and simmer until the pasta is done and has absorbed some of the sauce, about 2 minutes.

**VARIATION**

Ⓥ You can substitute medium shelled **shrimp** for the squid. *Cook the tomato sauce, covered, for about twenty minutes. Add the shrimp and cook until just done, about three minutes longer.*

**TEST-KITCHEN TIPS**

Squid must be braised slowly over low heat or cooked briefly over high heat. Anything in between makes rubber bands.

## wine recommendation

Given squid's mild flavor, the tomato sauce really dictates which wine to serve with this dish. Accordingly, a light-bodied, acidic red wine such as a young, slightly chilled Chianti will work just fine.

# farfalle with prosciutto, spinach, pine nuts and raisins

*The farfalle act like little shovels scooping up the pine nuts and raisins. Another pasta with the same facility, such as shells, will work equally well. Prosciutto and Parmesan add piquancy and saltiness to the dish, perfectly complementing the sweet raisins.*

**PREP TIME**
10 MINUTES

**COOK TIME**
15 MINUTES

**SERVES 4**

- ½ cup pine nuts
- ½ cup raisins
- ½ cup boiling water
- ½ cup olive oil
- 6 cloves garlic, minced
- 10 ounces spinach, large stems removed, leaves washed and cut crosswise into 1-inch strips
- 1 pound farfalle
- ¼ pound sliced prosciutto, cut crosswise into ¼-inch strips
- ½ teaspoon salt
- ½ teaspoon fresh-ground black pepper
- ⅓ cup grated Parmesan

**1.** In a small frying pan, toast the pine nuts over moderately low heat, stirring frequently, until golden brown, about 5 minutes. Or toast them in a 350° oven for 5 to 10 minutes.

**2.** Combine the raisins and the boiling water. Let stand until plump, about 10 minutes. Drain.

**3.** In a large frying pan, heat the oil over moderately low heat. Add the garlic and cook, stirring, for 1 minute. Stir in the spinach and cook, stirring, until just wilted, about 2 minutes.

**4.** In a large pot of boiling, salted water, cook the farfalle until just done, about 15 minutes. Drain. Toss with the pine nuts, raisins, spinach mixture, prosciutto, salt, pepper and Parmesan.

**VARIATIONS**

Ⓥ Replace the pine nuts with **walnuts.**
Ⓥ Substitute **Swiss chard** for the spinach.

## wine recommendation

A fragrant and spicy gewürztraminer from the Alto Adige makes an unlikely but tasty mate for this pasta.

# spaghetti with escarole and bacon

*Crisp bacon complements escarole so well that you may be tempted to sauté the greens in the bacon fat, but don't do it; the bacon will then overwhelm the greens completely. Use olive oil instead, which will bring all the flavors together.*

PREP TIME
5 MINUTES

COOK TIME
15 MINUTES

SERVES 4

¼  pound sliced bacon, cut crosswise into thin strips
2  tablespoons olive oil
3  cloves garlic, minced
¼  teaspoon red-pepper flakes
1½  teaspoons anchovy paste
1  head escarole (about 1½ pounds), leaves cut into ½-inch strips (about 3 quarts)
⅔  cup canned low-sodium chicken broth or homemade stock
½  teaspoon salt
¾  pound spaghetti
⅓  cup grated Parmesan, plus more for serving
1  tablespoon butter

**1.** In a large deep frying pan, cook the bacon over moderate heat until crisp. Remove the bacon with a slotted spoon. Pour off all the fat from the pan.

**2.** In the same pan, heat the oil over moderately low heat. Add the garlic, red-pepper flakes and anchovy paste and cook, stirring, until fragrant, about 30 seconds. Stir in the escarole, a little at a time, until wilted, about 3 minutes. Add the broth and ¼ teaspoon of the salt and bring to a simmer. Reduce the heat and cook, covered, for 5 minutes.

**3.** Meanwhile, in a large pot of boiling, salted water, cook the spaghetti until just done, about 12 minutes. Drain the pasta; add it to the pan with the escarole. Stir in the remaining ¼ teaspoon salt, the Parmesan, bacon and butter.

VARIATIONS

Ⓥ Stir in a cup of drained canned **cannellini beans** when you add the broth in Step 2.
Ⓥ Add two tablespoons of chopped fresh **basil** just before serving.

wine recommendation

Italian white wines were made for dishes like this one. Soave, Orvieto, Frascati—all are based on the trebbiano grape and have the crisp, neutral, refreshing taste and light body that allow the pasta to take center stage.

# orecchiette with broccoli rabe, bacon and bread crumbs

*For a pleasant change of pace, we toss crisp, golden bread crumbs with the pasta instead of the usual grated cheese. If you don't have orecchiette, replace them with shells, bow ties, rotelle or fusilli.*

**PREP TIME**
10 MINUTES

**COOK TIME**
20 MINUTES

**SERVES 4**

1   pound broccoli rabe, tough ends removed, cut into 1-inch lengths
½   cup olive oil
1   cup fresh bread crumbs
4   slices bacon, cut crosswise into ¼-inch strips
6   cloves garlic, minced
¼   teaspoon dried red-pepper flakes
1   pound orecchiette
¾   teaspoon salt

**1.** In a medium pot of boiling, salted water, cook the broccoli rabe until almost done, about 3 minutes. Drain thoroughly.

**2.** In a large nonstick frying pan, heat ¼ cup of the oil over moderate heat. Add the bread crumbs and cook, stirring, until golden, about 5 minutes. Remove. Wipe out the pan.

**3.** In the same pan, cook the bacon until crisp. Remove the bacon and drain on paper towels. Pour off all the fat. Heat the remaining ¼ cup oil in the frying pan over moderately low heat. Add the garlic and red-pepper flakes and cook, stirring, for 1 minute. Add the broccoli rabe and cook, stirring occasionally, until just done, about 3 minutes longer.

**4.** In a large pot of boiling, salted water, cook the orecchiette until done, about 15 minutes. Drain and toss with the bread crumbs, bacon, broccoli rabe and salt.

**FRESH BREAD CRUMBS**

The quickest way to make fresh bread crumbs is to tear up a few slices of French or Italian bread and whir them in the food processor. No need to remove the crust.

## wine recommendation

The bitter bite of the broccoli rabe and the pungent garlic in this dish both require a crisp white wine to act as a neutral foil. Try a pinot grigio from Friuli for good effect.

# fettuccine with veal, peas and mint

*With the veal scaloppine, peas and mint, this pasta is springlike, although you can make it year-round. Buy frozen petite peas, which are as good as—if not better than— what's usually available fresh and are a lot easier to prepare.*

**PREP TIME**
5 MINUTES

**COOK TIME**
20 MINUTES

**SERVES 4**

- 2 **tablespoons butter**
- 2 **tablespoons olive oil**
- ½ **pound veal scaloppine, cut into 1-by-2-inch strips**
- 1 **teaspoon salt**
- 1 **small onion, chopped fine**
- 2 **tablespoons dry vermouth or dry white wine**
- 1 **cup canned low-sodium chicken broth or homemade stock**
- 1 **cup heavy cream**
- 1 **cup frozen petite peas**
- ¾ **pound fettuccine**
- ¼ **teaspoon fresh-ground black pepper**
- ⅓ **cup lightly packed mint leaves, cut into thin strips**

**1.** In a large frying pan, melt 1 tablespoon of the butter with 1 tablespoon of the oil over moderately high heat. Add the veal and ¼ teaspoon of the salt and cook, turning, until just done, about 1 minute in all. Remove.

**2.** Reduce the heat to moderately low. Add the remaining 1 tablespoon oil and the onion. Cook, stirring occasionally, until translucent, about 5 minutes. Stir in the vermouth and then the broth and cream; bring to a simmer. Cook, stirring occasionally, until thickened, about 4 minutes. Add the peas and heat through, about 1 minute. Add the meat with any accumulated juices and the remaining ¾ teaspoon salt.

**3.** In a large pot of boiling, salted water, cook the fettuccine until just done, about 12 minutes. Drain. Toss with the sauce, the pepper, the remaining 1 tablespoon butter and the mint. Let sit for 2 to 3 minutes so that the pasta absorbs some of the sauce.

### FRESH MINT FLAVOR

Mint begins to lose flavor as soon as it's picked. Even if the bunch you're using looks fine, it may have been picked long enough ago so that the flavor is weak. Taste the sauce and, if you like, add more mint.

## wine recommendation

A light and acidic vinho verde from Portugal or a sauvignon blanc from the Loire Valley in France, such as a Pouilly-Fumé, will mirror the refreshing flavor of the mint.

# rigatoni with sausage and tomato cream sauce

*Tubes of rigatoni hold the tomato sauce, giving you a burst of creamy flavor with every bite. Use either hot or mild Italian sausage here, depending on your preference.*

**PREP TIME**
10 MINUTES

**COOK TIME**
30 MINUTES

**SERVES 4**

| | |
|---|---|
| 1 | tablespoon olive oil |
| 1½ | pounds mild or hot Italian sausage, casings removed |
| 1 | onion, chopped |
| 3 | cloves garlic, minced |
| ⅓ | cup dry white wine |
| 1½ | cups canned crushed tomatoes in thick puree (from a 15-ounce can) |
| ½ | teaspoon salt |
| ½ | teaspoon fresh-ground black pepper |
| ¼ | cup chopped fresh parsley |
| 1 | cup light cream |
| 1 | pound rigatoni |

Grated Parmesan, for serving

**1.** In a large frying pan, heat the oil over moderate heat. Add the sausage and cook, breaking up the meat with a fork, until it is no longer pink, about 5 minutes. With a slotted spoon, remove the sausage from the pan. Discard all but 1 tablespoon fat.

**2.** Reduce the heat to moderately low. Add the onion and garlic and cook, stirring occasionally, until the onion is translucent, about 5 minutes. Add the wine and cook until it almost evaporates, about 5 minutes. Stir in the sausage, tomatoes and salt. Simmer, covered, for 10 minutes. Add the pepper, parsley and cream.

**3.** In a large pot of boiling, salted water, cook the rigatoni until just done, about 14 minutes. Drain the pasta and toss with the sauce. Serve with grated Parmesan.

## wine recommendation

A Chianti Classico Riserva is the wine of choice with this dish. Look for a wine with a few years of age; it will be mellower and will complement the sauce better than a younger wine could.

# country-style rigatoni

*Sausage, escarole and white beans join chunky rigatoni in a garlicky broth slightly thickened with Parmesan. Don't stir too much after adding the beans, or they'll break up.*

**PREP TIME**
5 MINUTES

**COOK TIME**
20 MINUTES

**SERVES 4**

- 1 tablespoon cooking oil
- 1 pound mild or hot Italian sausage
- 3 cloves garlic, minced
- 2 cups canned low-sodium chicken broth or homemade stock
- 1 head escarole, torn into 2-inch pieces (about 2 quarts)
- 1 cup drained and rinsed canned cannellini beans (from one 15-ounce can)
- ⅓ cup grated Parmesan, plus more for serving
- ½ teaspoon salt
- ¼ teaspoon fresh-ground black pepper
- ¾ pound rigatoni

**1.** In a large deep frying pan, heat the oil over moderate heat. Add the sausage and cook, turning, until browned and cooked through, about 10 minutes. Remove. When the sausage is cool enough to handle, cut it into slices.

**2.** Put the garlic and the broth in the pan and bring to a simmer. Add the escarole, cover and simmer for 5 minutes. Gently stir in the sausage, beans, Parmesan, salt and pepper and simmer 1 minute longer.

**3.** Meanwhile, in a large pot of boiling, salted water, cook the pasta until just done, about 14 minutes. Drain and toss with the sauce. Serve with additional Parmesan.

### BEST BEANS

Many canned beans are overcooked during processing to the point of mush. We find, though, that the Goya company consistently delivers a nice firm bean that holds up to reheating without falling apart.

## wine recommendation

This simple country-style pasta will be right at home with a rustic red from Italy. Go for a flavor-packed but surprisingly inexpensive Salice Salentino from Apulia, the hot, sunny heel of Italy's boot.

# cavatelli with sardinian meat sauce

*Frozen cavatelli is better than dried. Since this shape is thick and doughy, the dried version tends to get overcooked on the outside before it's done inside. If you can't find cavatelli in the freezer section of your grocery store, a chunky dried pasta such as rigatoni will also be excellent here. Use the same quantity.*

**PREP TIME**
10 MINUTES

**COOK TIME**
25 MINUTES

**SERVES 4**

- 3 tablespoons olive oil
- ¾ pound hot Italian sausage, casings removed
- 1 onion, chopped
- 3 cloves garlic, minced
- 3 cups canned crushed tomatoes in thick puree (one 28-ounce can)
- 3 tablespoons chopped fresh mint (optional)
- ⅓ cup chopped fresh parsley
- ¼ cup water
- 1¼ teaspoons salt
- 2 large pinches saffron (optional)
- 1 pound frozen cavatelli
- ¼ cup chopped fresh basil
- 3 tablespoons grated Pecorino Romano or Parmesan, plus more for serving

**1.** In a large deep frying pan or Dutch oven, heat 1 tablespoon of the oil over moderate heat. Add the sausage and cook, breaking up the meat with a fork, until it is no longer pink, about 5 minutes.

**2.** Reduce the heat to moderately low and add the remaining 2 tablespoons oil to the pan. Stir in the onion and garlic. Cook, stirring occasionally, until the onion is translucent, about 5 minutes. Add the tomatoes, mint, parsley, water, salt and 1 pinch of the saffron. Simmer until thickened, about 15 minutes.

**3.** Meanwhile, in a large pot of boiling, salted water, cook the cavatelli with the remaining 1 pinch saffron until just done, 10 to 15 minutes. Reserve ½ cup of the pasta water. Drain the cavatelli and toss with the meat sauce, the basil, the reserved pasta water and the cheese. Serve with additional Pecorino Romano.

**VARIATIONS**

Ⓥ If you can't find hot Italian sausage, use **ground pork** or **mild sausage** and a quarter teaspoon of dried **red-pepper flakes.**

## wine recommendation

Red wines from Sardinia are almost impossible to find in the U.S., but a sturdy Cirò, made across the water in Calabria from the gaglioppo grape, will be a fine substitute.

RISOTTO WITH RADICCHIO AND SMOKED
MOZZARELLA, P. 86

4

# rice & polenta

# dried-porcini-mushroom risotto with goat cheese

*Using the mushroom-soaking liquid to cook the rice gives this risotto intense flavor. There's just enough goat cheese to balance the earthiness of the porcini with a touch of tartness without overwhelming the dish.*

**PREP TIME**
10 MINUTES

**COOK TIME**
35 MINUTES

**REST TIME**
20 MINUTES

**SERVES 4**

|   |   |
|---|---|
| 1 | cup dried porcini or other dried mushrooms (about 1 ounce) |
| 3 | cups hot water, more if needed |
| 3½ | cups canned low-sodium chicken broth or homemade stock, more if needed |
| 3 | tablespoons olive oil |
| 1 | onion, chopped |
| 5 | cloves garlic, minced |
| 2 | cups arborio rice |
| 1¼ | teaspoons salt |
| 2 | tablespoons butter |
| ¼ | teaspoon fresh-ground black pepper |
| 2 | ounces mild goat cheese, such as Montrachet, crumbled |

Grated Parmesan, for serving

**1.** Put the dried mushrooms in a medium bowl and pour the hot water over them. Soak until softened, about 20 minutes. Remove the mushrooms, reserving the soaking liquid, and chop them. Strain the liquid through a paper-towel-lined sieve into a medium saucepan. Add the broth to the pan and bring to a simmer.

**2.** In a medium pot, heat the oil over moderately low heat. Add the onion and garlic and cook, stirring occasionally, until the onion is translucent, about 5 minutes. Add the chopped mushrooms, the rice and the salt and stir until the rice begins to turn opaque, about 2 minutes.

**3.** Add about ½ cup of the simmering broth to the rice and cook, stirring frequently, until the broth has been completely absorbed. The rice and broth should bubble gently; adjust the heat as needed. Continue cooking the rice, adding broth ½ cup at a time and allowing the rice to absorb it before adding the next ½ cup. Cook the rice in this way until tender, 25 to 30 minutes in all. The broth that hasn't been absorbed should be thickened by the starch from the rice. You may not need to use all of the liquid, or you may need more broth or some water.

**4.** Stir in the butter, pepper and goat cheese. Serve the risotto with grated Parmesan.

## wine recommendation

Tuscany's chardonnays, loaded with tropical fruit flavors and generously oaked, are not typically Italian. No matter; they have the power and concentration to make a great combination here.

# risotto with radicchio and smoked mozzarella

*Mellow, melting cubes of smoked mozzarella balance the slightly bitter radicchio perfectly. You can use curly endive in place of the radicchio, if you prefer, or escarole if you want to eliminate the bitterness. Substitute salted mozzarella if smoked is not available.*

**PREP TIME**
10 MINUTES

**COOK TIME**
35 MINUTES

**SERVES 4**

- 5 cups canned low-sodium chicken broth or homemade stock, more if needed
- 1 cup water, more if needed
- 2 tablespoons olive oil
- 1 onion, chopped
- 2 cups arborio rice
- ½ cup dry white wine
- 1¾ teaspoons salt
- 1 head radicchio (about ½ pound), cut into 1-inch pieces
- 3 tablespoons chopped fresh parsley
- ¼ teaspoon fresh-ground black pepper
- 2 tablespoons butter
- ½ pound smoked mozzarella, cut into ¼-inch dice

**1.** In a medium saucepan, bring the broth and water to a simmer. In a large pot, heat the oil over moderately low heat. Add the onion and cook, stirring occasionally, until translucent, about 5 minutes.

**2.** Add the rice to the pot and stir until it begins to turn opaque, about 2 minutes. Add the wine and salt and cook, stirring frequently, until all the wine has been absorbed.

**3.** Add about ½ cup of the simmering broth to the rice and cook, stirring frequently, until the broth has been completely absorbed. The rice and broth should bubble gently; adjust the heat as needed. Continue cooking the rice, adding broth ½ cup at a time and allowing the rice to absorb the broth before adding the next ½ cup. Cook the rice in this way until almost tender, about 20 minutes in all. Add the radicchio and parsley and cook until the radicchio and the rice are tender, about 5 minutes more. The broth that hasn't been absorbed should be thickened by the starch from the rice. You may not need to use all of the liquid, or you may need more broth or some water.

**4.** Stir the pepper and the butter into the risotto. Add the mozzarella and stir until it melts into a web.

## wine recommendation

Here's a risotto that can stand up to red wine. Try an unoaked Barbera d'Alba, a lively and fruity wine with very light tannins that won't accentuate the bitterness of the radicchio.

# "sicilian" rice salad

*All right, we confess, this recipe isn't really from Sicily—we just invented it ourselves. But there's no denying the southern Italian heritage of the ingredients, and, like much of the region's cooking, our "Sicilian" salad is bold in flavor.*

**PREP TIME**
5 MINUTES

**COOK TIME**
10 MINUTES

**SERVES 4**

1½ cups rice
¼ cup pine nuts
⅓ cup drained and chopped oil-packed sun-dried tomatoes
2 tablespoons drained capers
⅓ cup chopped red onion (about ½ small onion)
1 6-ounce can tuna, drained
1 2-ounce tin anchovy fillets, drained and minced
¼ cup olive oil
1 tablespoon lemon juice
2 tablespoons red- or white-wine vinegar
¾ teaspoon salt
½ teaspoon fresh-ground black pepper
¼ cup thin-sliced basil or mint leaves

**1.** Bring a medium pot of salted water to a boil. Stir in the rice and boil until just done, 10 to 12 minutes. Drain. Rinse with cold water and drain thoroughly. Put the rice in a large glass or stainless-steel bowl.

**2.** Meanwhile, in a small frying pan, toast the pine nuts over moderately low heat, stirring frequently, until golden brown, about 5 minutes. Or toast the pine nuts in a 350° oven for 5 to 10 minutes.

**3.** Stir the toasted pine nuts, the sun-dried tomatoes, capers, onion, tuna and anchovies into the rice. Toss the rice salad with the oil, lemon juice, vinegar, salt, pepper and basil.

**VARIATIONS**

**V** If you'd like more anchovy flavor, use some of the **oil** from the **anchovy tin** in place of some of the olive oil.
**V** Add a handful of chopped pitted **green** or **black olives.**

## wine recommendation

The wine scene on the sun-baked island of Sicily is dominated by a few large players, one of which is the firm of Regaleali. Their inexpensive rosé is a delight and an appropriate choice for this salad.

# rice salad with chicken and asparagus

*The rice soaks up the dressing as the salad sits, so if you make it more than half an hour ahead, it may dry out. In that case, just add some extra oil and lemon juice.*

**PREP TIME**
10 MINUTES

**COOK TIME**
30 MINUTES

**SERVES 4**

⅓  cup pine nuts
5  tablespoons wine vinegar
1  clove garlic, minced
1  tablespoon lemon juice
1  tablespoon Dijon mustard
2  teaspoons salt
¾  teaspoon fresh-ground black pepper
9  tablespoons olive oil
2  cups rice, preferably arborio
1  pound asparagus, tough ends snapped off and discarded, stems cut into ¼-inch pieces, tips left whole
1⅓  pounds boneless chicken thighs (about 6)
1  large tomato, cut into ½-inch dice
½  cup chopped red onion

**1.** In a small frying pan, toast the pine nuts over moderately low heat, stirring frequently, until they are golden brown, about 5 minutes. Or toast in a 350° oven for 5 to 10 minutes.

**2.** In a small glass or stainless-steel bowl, using a fork, stir together the vinegar, garlic, lemon juice, mustard, 1¼ teaspoons of the salt and ½ teaspoon of the pepper. Stir in the oil.

**3.** In a large pot of boiling, salted water, cook the rice until almost tender, about 10 minutes. Add the asparagus and cook until it and the rice are both done, about 5 minutes longer. Drain, rinse with cold water and drain again. Transfer to a large glass or stainless-steel bowl.

**4.** Meanwhile, in a large frying pan, bring ¼ inch of water to a simmer over moderately high heat. Sprinkle the chicken with the remaining ¾ teaspoon salt and ¼ teaspoon pepper and add to the pan. Cover, reduce the heat and simmer, turning once, until cooked through, about 8 minutes. Remove the chicken, let cool slightly and then cut into ½-inch chunks. Add to the rice and asparagus.

**5.** Add the tomato and red onion to the rice and then toss the salad with the dressing. Stir in the pine nuts just before serving.

## wine recommendation

Vinegar and asparagus are hard to match with wine, but sauvignon blanc can handle both. Look for one from Friuli or Alto Adige.

# polenta with eggplant, onion and tomatoes

*Sauté onion, eggplant and tomatoes with plenty of garlic for a combination reminiscent of ratatouille. Then spoon this tasty vegetable stew over steaming Parmesan polenta to make a satisfying meal.*

**PREP TIME**
10 MINUTES

**COOK TIME**
45 MINUTES

**SERVES 4**

- 10 tablespoons olive oil
- 1 onion, chopped
- 5 cloves garlic, minced
- 1 large eggplant (about 1¾ pounds), cut into ½-inch cubes
- 2 tomatoes (about ¾ pound), cut into ½-inch pieces
- 1 cup canned crushed tomatoes in thick puree
- 3 tablespoons chopped fresh parsley
- 2¼ teaspoons salt
- ¼ teaspoon fresh-ground black pepper
- 4½ cups water
- 1⅓ cups coarse or medium cornmeal
- 6 tablespoons grated Parmesan

**1.** In a large nonstick frying pan, heat 1 tablespoon of the oil over moderate heat. Add the onion and garlic and cook, stirring occasionally, until the onion starts to brown, about 5 minutes. Remove. Heat 6 tablespoons of the oil in the same pan over moderately high heat. Add the eggplant and cook, stirring occasionally, until golden, about 10 minutes. Add the onion mixture, fresh and canned tomatoes, parsley and 1 teaspoon of the salt. Simmer until thick, about 10 minutes. Stir in the pepper.

**2.** Meanwhile, in a medium saucepan, bring the water and the remaining 1¼ teaspoons salt to a boil. Add the cornmeal in a slow stream, whisking constantly. Whisk in the remaining 3 tablespoons oil. Reduce the heat and simmer, stirring frequently with a wooden spoon, until the polenta is thick, about 20 minutes. Stir in the Parmesan. Serve the hot polenta topped with the vegetables.

## wine recommendation

A hearty dish needs a hearty wine. Open an earthy Salice Salentino from Dr. Cosimo Taurino. Made from the obscure negro amaro grape, it is one of the best wines from Italy's Apulia region.

# polenta with meat sauce

*This is comfort food at its finest: a quick-cooking Bolognese sauce, made with sausage, tomatoes, aromatic vegetables and a touch of light cream, served over a mound of earthy polenta. Of course, you could put the same sauce over fettuccine instead.*

**PREP TIME**
15 MINUTES

**COOK TIME**
50 MINUTES

**SERVES 4**

| | |
|---|---|
| 4 | tablespoons olive oil |
| 1½ | pounds mild Italian sausage, casings removed |
| 2 | carrots, chopped |
| 1 | onion, chopped |
| 4 | cloves garlic, minced |
| ⅓ | cup dry white wine |
| 1½ | cups canned crushed tomatoes in thick puree (from a 15-ounce can) |
| ¾ | cup canned low-sodium chicken broth or homemade stock |
| 6 | tablespoons chopped fresh parsley |
| 1 | bay leaf |
| 1¾ | teaspoons salt |
| ¼ | teaspoon fresh-ground black pepper |
| 3 | tablespoons light cream |
| 4½ | cups water |
| 1⅓ | cups coarse or medium cornmeal |
| 3 | tablespoons grated Parmesan, plus more for serving |

**1.** In a large deep frying pan, heat 1 tablespoon of the oil over moderately high heat. Add the sausage and cook, breaking up the meat with a fork, until no longer pink, about 3 minutes. Tilt the pan and spoon off all but 2 tablespoons fat. Reduce the heat to moderate. Add the carrots, onion and garlic and cook, stirring occasionally, until the vegetables start to soften, about 5 minutes.

**2.** Stir in the wine and let simmer 3 minutes. Add the tomatoes, broth, 4 tablespoons of the parsley, the bay leaf and ½ teaspoon of the salt. Simmer, covered, for 15 minutes. Uncover, add the pepper and simmer 5 minutes longer. Remove the bay leaf. Stir in the cream and the remaining 2 tablespoons parsley.

**3.** Meanwhile, in a medium saucepan, bring the water and the remaining 1¼ teaspoons salt to a boil. Add the cornmeal in a slow stream, whisking constantly. Whisk in the remaining 3 tablespoons oil. Reduce the heat and simmer, stirring frequently with a wooden spoon, until the polenta is thick, about 20 minutes. Stir in the Parmesan.

**4.** Serve the polenta topped with the meat sauce. Pass additional Parmesan.

## wine recommendation

Homey food calls for a simple but flavorful red wine. For a touch of regional authenticity, select a Sangiovese di Romagna.

BRAISED PORK WITH BACON AND ONIONS, P. 114

# 5

# *on the stove*

# cauliflower, bacon and parmesan frittata

*Eggs make perfect weeknight dinners; they cook quickly and taste great with an endless variety of ingredients. Here, bacon, sautéed cauliflower and grated Parmesan complement each other in an original and satisfying frittata.*

**PREP TIME**
10 MINUTES

**COOK TIME**
35 MINUTES

**SERVES 4**

- ¼ pound bacon, slices cut crosswise into ¼-inch strips
- 8 large eggs
- ⅓ cup light cream
- 1 cup grated Parmesan
- 3 tablespoons chopped fresh parsley
- ⅛ teaspoon fresh-ground black pepper
- 2 tablespoons olive oil
- 1 tablespoon butter
- 1 small head cauliflower (about 1¼ pounds), cut into small florets
- ¼ teaspoon salt
- 4 cloves garlic, minced

**1.** In a 10-inch nonstick frying pan, cook the bacon until crisp. Remove. Pour off all the fat. In a large bowl, beat the eggs with the cream, Parmesan, parsley and pepper until smooth. Add the cooled bacon.

**2.** In the same frying pan, heat the oil with the butter over moderately high heat. Add the cauliflower and salt and cook, stirring occasionally, until the cauliflower is golden and almost done, 10 to 15 minutes. Add the garlic and cook, stirring, 1 minute longer. Pour in the egg mixture and reduce the heat to low. Cook, covered, until the bottom of the frittata is golden brown and the top is almost set, 10 to 15 minutes.

**3.** Heat the broiler. Broil the frittata 6 inches from the heat, if possible, until the eggs are set and beginning to brown, about 3 minutes.

**4.** Lift up the edge of the frittata with a spatula and slide the frittata onto a plate. Cut it into wedges.

**TEST-KITCHEN TIP**

If the handle of your frying pan isn't ovenproof, you can make it so. Protect it from the heat of the broiler by wrapping it with four layers of aluminum foil.

## wine recommendation

Cheese and eggs both work well with red wine; their richness blunts the wine's tannin, while accentuating its fruitiness. A simple Chianti or Chianti Classico will be delightful.

# garlic shrimp in tomato sauce

*Chunky with capers and olives, this quick tomato sauce tastes much like the familiar* puttanesca *sauce that is usually served on pasta. We use it to coat shrimp sautéed with garlic and hot pepper.*

**PREP TIME**
15 MINUTES

**COOK TIME**
20 MINUTES

**SERVES 4**

- 3 tablespoons olive oil
- 2 pounds large shrimp, shelled
- 4 cloves garlic, minced
- 1 large pinch dried red-pepper flakes
- ¼ teaspoon salt
- ¼ teaspoon fresh-ground black pepper
- 2 medium tomatoes (about ¾ pound), peeled and chopped
- 1 cup canned crushed tomatoes in thick puree
- 1 teaspoon chopped fresh rosemary, or ¼ teaspoon dried rosemary
- 2 tablespoons drained capers
- ⅓ cup halved and pitted black olives

**1.** In a large nonstick frying pan, heat the oil over moderate heat. Add the shrimp, garlic, red-pepper flakes, salt and black pepper and cook, stirring occasionally, until the shrimp are just done, about 5 minutes. Remove the shrimp with a slotted spoon.

**2.** Add the fresh tomatoes, canned tomatoes, rosemary, capers and olives to the pan. Reduce the heat and simmer, covered, for 15 minutes. Stir in the shrimp and simmer until just heated through, about 1 minute.

**VARIATION**

🅥 Substitute four boneless, skinless **chicken breasts** for the shrimp. *Make the sauce separately by sautéing the garlic for a minute, adding the red-pepper flakes, salt and black pepper, and then proceeding with Step 2. In a medium frying pan, heat just one tablespoon of oil over moderate heat. Season the chicken breasts with a quarter teaspoon salt and an eighth teaspoon pepper and put them in the pan. Cook the chicken until brown, about five minutes. Turn and cook until almost done, about three minutes longer. Cover the pan, remove from the heat and let steam five minutes. Top the chicken with the sauce.*

## wine recommendation

A smooth, medium-bodied red from southern Italy, such as a Cirò or Regaleali Rosso, will stand up to the gutsy sauce without overpowering the shrimp.

# mediterranean rice salad with seared tuna

*With its tomato, red bell pepper, black olives, thyme and tuna, this salad sings of the sunny Mediterranean. Boiling the rice rather than steaming it cuts down the cooking time considerably.*

**PREP TIME**
10 MINUTES

**COOK TIME**
15 MINUTES

**SERVES 4**

1½ cups long-grain rice
1 small red onion, chopped
1 large tomato, seeded and cut into ½-inch dice
1 red bell pepper, seeds and ribs removed, cut into ½-inch dice
½ cup black olives, such as kalamata, halved and pitted
3 tablespoons chopped flat-leaf parsley
1 teaspoon dried thyme
3 tablespoons white-wine vinegar
1½ teaspoons Dijon mustard
1 clove garlic, minced
1½ teaspoons salt
¾ teaspoon fresh-ground black pepper
⅓ cup plus 1 tablespoon olive oil
4 tuna steaks, about ½ inch thick (1½ pounds in all)

**1.** In a large pot of boiling, salted water, cook the rice until just done, about 10 minutes. Drain. Rinse with cold water. Drain thoroughly.

**2.** In a medium glass or stainless-steel bowl, combine the rice, onion, tomato, bell pepper, olives, parsley and ½ teaspoon of the thyme. In a small glass or stainless-steel bowl, whisk the vinegar with the mustard, garlic, 1 teaspoon of the salt and ½ teaspoon of the black pepper. Add the ⅓ cup oil slowly, whisking. Toss this vinaigrette with the rice mixture.

**3.** Rub the tuna with the remaining 1 tablespoon oil and sprinkle with the remaining ½ teaspoon thyme, ½ teaspoon salt and ¼ teaspoon black pepper. Heat a grill pan or large heavy frying pan over moderately high heat. Put the tuna in the pan and cook for 2 minutes. Turn and cook until done to your taste, about 2 minutes longer for medium rare. Mound the rice salad on plates and top with the tuna.

## wine recommendation

Look for a light, refreshing white wine from the Mediterranean. Either a bottle of the delightful albariño from Galicia in Spain or a Côtes de Gascogne from southwestern France would be appropriate.

# steamed mussels with tomato-and-garlic broth

*Mussels have three things going for them: They're cheap, quick to cook and delicious. Using clean farmed mussels negates their one big drawback— the tedious chore of scrubbing and debearding.*

**PREP TIME**
10 MINUTES

**COOK TIME**
35 MINUTES

**SERVES 4**

¼ cup olive oil
1 onion, chopped fine
6 cloves garlic, minced
3 tablespoons chopped fresh parsley
2 cups drained canned tomatoes in thick puree (from a 28-ounce can), chopped
¼ teaspoon dried thyme
¼ teaspoon dried red-pepper flakes
4 pounds mussels, scrubbed and debearded
⅛ teaspoon fresh-ground black pepper
Salt, if needed
Garlic Toast, *opposite* (optional)

**1.** In a large pot, heat the oil over moderately low heat. Add the onion and garlic and cook, stirring occasionally, until the onion is translucent, about 5 minutes. Stir in the parsley, tomatoes, thyme and red-pepper flakes. Reduce the heat and simmer, partially covered, for 25 minutes, stirring occasionally.

**2.** Discard any mussels that have broken shells or that don't clamp shut when tapped. Add the mussels to the pot. Cover; bring to a boil. Cook, shaking the pot occasionally, just until the mussels open, about 3 minutes. Remove the open mussels. Continue to boil, uncovering the pot as necessary to remove the mussels as soon as their shells open. Discard any that do not open.

**3.** Stir the black pepper into the broth. Taste the broth and, if needed, add salt. Ladle the broth over the mussels and serve with the Garlic Toast.

**GARLIC TOAST**

4 ½-inch-thick slices country bread
1 clove garlic, halved

Heat the broiler. Put the bread on a baking sheet and broil, turning once, until crisp and brown on the outside but still slightly soft in the center, about 3 minutes. Rub one side of each slice with the cut-side of the garlic.

## wine recommendation

Every Mediterranean country has its version of shellfish in a tomato-based broth, and the wine of choice for each is an earthy, full-bodied pink wine. Here, seek out a Lacryma Christi rosé.

# sautéed whole trout with sage and white wine

*The garnish of fried sage leaves makes a delectable crisp treat, but of course the trout is still good without it. You can usually sauté four small trout at the same time in a large frying pan, but if they're crowded, cook the fish in two pans or two batches.*

**COOK TIME**
20 MINUTES

**SERVES 4**

- 4  trout (about ¾ pound each), cleaned
- 3  tablespoons olive oil
- 5  tablespoons cold butter

Salt

Fresh-ground black pepper

About 36 fresh sage leaves, or 1 teaspoon dried sage

- ⅓  cup dry white wine

**1.** Rinse the fish and dry the surface and the cavity of each thoroughly with paper towels. In a large nonstick frying pan, heat 2 tablespoons of the oil with 1 tablespoon of the butter over moderately high heat. Sprinkle the trout with ½ teaspoon salt and ¼ teaspoon pepper. Put the trout in the pan and cook until golden, about 5 minutes. Turn and cook until golden on the second side and just done, 5 to 10 minutes longer. Remove; wipe out the pan.

**2.** In the same pan, heat the remaining 1 tablespoon oil over moderately high heat. Add the sage leaves and cook until crisp, about 1 minute. Alternatively, add the dried sage and cook, stirring, for 1 minute. Pour the oil and sage over the fish. Wipe out the pan.

**3.** Add the wine to the pan. Boil until reduced to approximately 3 tablespoons, 1 to 2 minutes. Reduce the heat to the lowest setting and whisk in the remaining 4 tablespoons butter, ⅛ teaspoon salt and ⅛ teaspoon pepper. Whisk in any accumulated juices and oil from the trout. Pour the sauce around the fish and serve.

**TEST-KITCHEN TIP**

For a creamy emulsified butter sauce, don't just put the butter in the pan and let it melt; instead, stick a whisk in the cold butter and stir it around the bottom of the pan over the lowest possible heat. This way, the butter just softens into a sauce instead of melting into a puddle.

## wine recommendation

Farm-raised trout are mild, so a pinot grigio or pinot bianco from northeastern Italy will make a superb accompaniment. A gamier wild fish can use a stronger wine such as a chardonnay.

# braised chicken thighs with olives and basil

*Though it cooks for only half an hour, this dish has the satisfying, melded flavor of a long-simmered stew. Part of the explanation is that the garlic cloves are cooked whole and then mashed into the sauce. You'll always get a more mellow flavor from whole cloves than from chopped or crushed garlic.*

**PREP TIME**
10 MINUTES

**COOK TIME**
35 MINUTES

**SERVES 4**

- 1 tablespoon olive oil
- 8 chicken thighs (about 3 pounds in all)
- 1 teaspoon salt
- Fresh-ground black pepper
- 1 onion, chopped
- 12 cloves garlic, peeled
- 2 teaspoons chopped fresh rosemary, or ¾ teaspoon dried rosemary
- ½ cup dry white wine
- ½ cup canned low-sodium chicken broth or homemade stock
- 1 cup canned crushed tomatoes in thick puree
- ⅓ cup halved and pitted black olives
- ⅓ cup chopped fresh basil

**1.** In a large deep frying pan, heat the oil over moderately high heat. Season the chicken with ½ teaspoon of the salt and ¼ teaspoon pepper. Put the chicken in the pan and brown well on both sides, about 8 minutes in all. Remove. Pour off all but 1 tablespoon of the fat. Reduce the heat to moderately low.

**2.** Add the onion and garlic and cook, stirring occasionally, until the onion starts to soften, about 5 minutes. Add the rosemary and wine. Bring to a simmer, scraping the bottom of the pan to dislodge any brown bits. Boil until the wine is reduced to approximately ¼ cup, 1 to 2 minutes.

**3.** Add the broth, tomatoes, olives, the remaining ½ teaspoon salt and the chicken, skin-side up, with any accumulated juices. Cover and simmer until the chicken is just done, 20 to 25 minutes. Push the chicken to the side of the pan and then mash the garlic cloves with a fork. Stir in ⅛ teaspoon pepper and the basil, bring just to a simmer and serve.

## wine recommendation

Italy has three great red grapes. Nebbiolo and sangiovese are well known, but the robust aglianico grape deserves at least the same regard. This dish is a great opportunity to sample either of its best wines, Taurasi or Aglianico del Vulture.

# veal chops milanese with sage

*To get half-inch veal chops, the butcher will have to cut two chops per rib rather than just cutting between ribs. Half of the chops will have a rib bone and half won't. Ask the butcher to pound the chops for you to an eighth of an inch thick, or do the flattening at home with a meat pounder or the bottom of a heavy frying pan.*

**PREP TIME**
15 MINUTES

**COOK TIME**
7 MINUTES

**SERVES 4**

- 1  egg
- ¼  teaspoon salt
- ⅛  teaspoon fresh-ground black pepper
- ¾  cup fine dry bread crumbs
- 1  tablespoon chopped fresh sage, or 1 teaspoon dried sage
- 4  ½-inch-thick veal rib chops (about 5 ounces each), chine bone removed, chops pounded to ⅛ inch thick
- 5  tablespoons butter
- 1  lemon, cut into wedges

**1.** Beat the egg to mix with the salt and the pepper. Combine the bread crumbs and the fresh or dried sage. Dip the veal chops (including the rib bone if the chop has one) into the beaten egg and then into the bread crumbs. Shake off the excess bread crumbs.

**2.** In a large nonstick frying pan, melt the butter over moderately low heat. Put the coated veal chops in the pan and cook until golden, about 4 minutes. Turn and cook until golden and just done, about 3 minutes longer. Serve with the lemon wedges.

**VARIATIONS**

Ⓥ These chops are also excellent, and in fact more traditional, **without the sage.**

Ⓥ You can throw tradition to the winds and sauté the chops **without pounding.** They'll need another minute of cooking per side.

Ⓥ Another possibility is to make this with **pork chops,** either pounded or not.

**TEST-KITCHEN TIP**

To ensure a crisp coating, keep the heat steady at moderately low. Don't be tempted to turn it down or the crumbs won't brown to a crunchy gold.

## wine recommendation

Try a Sankt Magdalener riesling or, if you can't find one, a German kabinett halbtrocken riesling. You'll be happily surprised by how good the combination of the wine and the veal chops will taste.

# lamb chops with rosemary and grapes

*You'd expect to find lamb chops grilled with rosemary, but the sauce—a fruity mixture of grapes, white wine and just a touch of honey—is a delightful surprise. You'll want to choose seedless grapes for this recipe.*

**PREP TIME**
5 MINUTES

**COOK TIME**
20 MINUTES

**SERVES 4**

1½  tablespoons olive oil
 8  lamb loin chops, about
     1¼ inches thick
     (about 3 pounds in all)
Salt
Fresh-ground black pepper
 3  tablespoons chopped
     fresh rosemary
 4  cloves garlic, cut into
     thin slices
 2  cups red grapes
     (from about a
     1-pound bunch)
⅓  cup dry white wine
 1  teaspoon honey

**1.** In a large stainless-steel or nonstick frying pan, heat the oil over moderately high heat. Season the lamb chops with ½ teaspoon salt and ¼ teaspoon pepper. Put the chops in the pan and sprinkle 1½ tablespoons of the rosemary in the spaces between the chops. Cook the chops for 5 minutes. Turn and sprinkle the garlic in between the chops. Cook the chops until done to your taste, 3 to 5 minutes longer for medium rare.

**2.** Remove the chops and garlic and keep in a warm spot. Pour off all but 2 tablespoons of the fat from the pan. Add the grapes and the remaining 1½ tablespoons rosemary to the pan. Reduce the heat and cook, stirring frequently, until the grapes soften, about 8 minutes.

**3.** Add the wine to the pan and simmer 2 minutes. Stir in the garlic and any juices from the lamb, the honey, ⅛ teaspoon salt and a pinch of pepper. Serve the lamb topped with the grapes and sauce.

**VARIATION**

**Ⓥ** In place of the loin chops, you can use **lamb shoulder chops,** about one inch thick (about two pounds in all). Cook them a little less than the loin chops.

## wine recommendation

Cabernet sauvignon is classic with lamb, but a European cabernet will taste austere against the slightly sweet sauce here. Instead, try a California or Washington State cabernet, which will be fruity enough to blend with the sweetness.

# braised pork with bacon and onions

*Certain dishes of northeast Italy, such as this one, are influenced by the region's proximity to Austria and Germany. The somewhat acidic flavor of the pork is similar to that of German sauerbraten, but the garlic and rosemary add a distinctly Italian touch.*

**PREP TIME**
10 MINUTES

**COOK TIME**
35 MINUTES

**SERVES 4**

- 2 slices bacon, cut crosswise into ½-inch strips
- 2 pork tenderloins (about 1¾ pounds in all)
- Salt
- ½ teaspoon fresh-ground black pepper
- 1 tablespoon olive oil
- 2 onions, sliced thin
- 2 cloves garlic, minced
- ½ cup dry white wine
- 1 cup canned low-sodium chicken broth or homemade stock
- 1 teaspoon wine vinegar
- 3 cloves
- 2 bay leaves
- 1 sprig rosemary, or ½ teaspoon dried rosemary, crumbled

**1.** In a large deep stainless-steel frying pan or a Dutch oven, cook the bacon over moderate heat until crisp. Remove with a slotted spoon. Season the pork with ½ teaspoon salt and ¼ teaspoon of the pepper. Increase the heat to moderately high. Put the pork in the pan and brown on all sides, turning, about 8 minutes in all. Remove.

**2.** Reduce the heat to moderate and add the oil to the pan. Add the onions and garlic and cook, stirring occasionally, until the onions are golden, about 5 minutes. Add the wine and simmer for 3 minutes.

**3.** Stir in the broth, vinegar, cloves, bay leaves, rosemary, ¼ teaspoon salt and the pork with any accumulated juices. Bring to a simmer. Cover and simmer, turning the meat once, until the pork is just done, about 10 minutes. Remove the meat from the pan, transfer to a carving board and leave to rest in a warm spot for 5 minutes. Stir the remaining ¼ teaspoon pepper and ⅛ teaspoon salt into the pan and simmer until the sauce thickens slightly, about 3 minutes. Remove the cloves, bay leaves and rosemary sprig and stir in the bacon. Cut the meat into thin slices and serve topped with the sauce.

## wine recommendation

In Austria, Germany or Alsace, the classic accompaniment for this type of dish is gewürztraminer. Look for one of the superb examples from the Alto Adige or Germany's Pfalz region and you'll understand why.

# pork chops with marsala and fennel

*Thin slices of fennel, a shot of dry marsala and a touch of tomato paste combine to make a quick, intense pan sauce for sautéed pork chops. If you prefer, substitute red wine for the marsala.*

**PREP TIME**
10 MINUTES

**COOK TIME**
35 MINUTES

**SERVES 4**

- 1 tablespoon olive oil, more if needed
- 4 pork chops, about ¾ inch thick (about 2½ pounds in all)

Salt

Fresh-ground black pepper

- 1 onion, chopped
- 1 fennel bulb, cut into thin slices
- 4 cloves garlic, minced
- ½ cup dry marsala
- ⅔ cup canned low-sodium chicken broth or homemade stock
- 1 tablespoon tomato paste
- 3 tablespoons chopped fresh parsley

**1.** In a large frying pan, heat the oil over moderate heat. Season the pork chops with ¼ teaspoon each salt and pepper. Put the chops in the pan. Cook, turning once, until browned and done to medium, about 5 minutes per side. Remove and put in a warm place.

**2.** If necessary, add oil to the pan to make about 2 tablespoons fat. Add the onion, fennel and ⅛ teaspoon salt. Cook, covered, stirring occasionally, until soft, about 10 minutes. Uncover and add the garlic. Cook, stirring, 1 minute longer. Add the marsala. Bring to a boil, scraping the bottom of the pan to dislodge any brown bits. Boil until reduced to approximately ¼ cup, 1 to 2 minutes.

**3.** Stir in the broth, tomato paste, 2 tablespoons of the parsley, ½ teaspoon salt and any accumulated juices from the meat. Bring to a simmer and cook, covered, until the sauce thickens and the fennel is tender, about 5 minutes. Add the remaining 1 tablespoon parsley, ⅛ teaspoon pepper and the pork chops. Cook until just heated through, 2 to 3 minutes.

**VARIATION**

**V** Instead of chops, sauté one-inch-thick medallions of **pork tenderloin,** seasoned with salt and pepper, until just done, about two minutes per side.

## wine recommendation

A well-made Nebbiolo delle Langhe has earthy and herbal flavors to blend nicely with fennel and just the right amount of tannin and dried-cherry fruitiness for the marsala and pork.

# sausages, potatoes and artichoke hearts in tomato broth

*Simmering chunks of potato, Italian sausages and artichoke hearts in a tomatoey broth melds their flavors into a savory stew. Sop up the plentiful broth with crusty bread.*

**PREP TIME**
10 MINUTES

**COOK TIME**
50 MINUTES

**SERVES 4**

- 1 tablespoon olive oil
- 1½ pounds mild Italian sausages
- 3 cloves garlic, cut into thin slices
- 1½ pounds boiling potatoes (about 5), cut into 1-inch chunks
- ½ teaspoon dried thyme
- ⅓ cup dry white wine
- 1¼ cups canned low-sodium chicken broth or homemade stock
- 1 cup canned crushed tomatoes in thick puree
- 1½ cups drained and rinsed halved canned artichoke hearts (one 14-ounce can)
- 6 tablespoons chopped fresh parsley
- ½ teaspoon salt
- ½ teaspoon fresh-ground black pepper

**1.** In a large stainless-steel pot, heat the oil over moderately high heat. Add the sausages and brown well, about 10 minutes. Remove. Pour off all but 1 tablespoon of the fat.

**2.** Reduce the heat to moderate. Add the garlic, potatoes and thyme. Cook, stirring occasionally, until the potatoes are lightly browned, about 5 minutes. Add the wine and boil until reduced to approximately 3 tablespoons, 2 to 3 minutes.

**3.** Stir in the broth, tomatoes, artichoke hearts, 4 tablespoons of the parsley, the salt and the sausages. Bring to a simmer and cook, partially covered, until the potatoes are tender, about 30 minutes. Add the remaining 2 tablespoons parsley and the pepper.

**VARIATIONS**

Substitute:
- **Ⓥ Rosemary** for the thyme
- **Ⓥ Red wine** for the white wine
- **Ⓥ Hot Italian sausage** for the mild

## wine recommendation

This dish suggests cabernet sauvignon or sangiovese as a wine partner. You can have both in Carmignano, a rich Tuscan red based on the two grapes. Many good Chianti Classicos also have a high percentage of cabernet sauvignon and will work well here.

# sautéed steaks with red wine and peppers

*Chuck steaks have a full beefy flavor and stay remarkably tender when cooked to a rosy medium rare. If you like steaks well done, though, choose a different cut or the meat will be chewy. The red wine is meant to flavor the onion and peppers, not to make a sauce. Boil it until it's completely absorbed by the vegetables.*

**PREP TIME**
10 MINUTES

**COOK TIME**
20 MINUTES

**SERVES 4**

- 4 tablespoons olive oil
- 1 large onion, sliced thin
- 1½ teaspoons dried oregano
- 1 large clove garlic, minced
- 1 red bell pepper, sliced thin
- 1 green bell pepper, sliced thin
- 4 top chuck steaks (about 2 pounds in all), pounded to ½ inch thick
- 1 teaspoon salt
- ¾ teaspoon fresh-ground black pepper
- ¾ cup red wine

**1.** Heat 2 tablespoons of the oil in a medium frying pan over moderately low heat. Stir in the onion, oregano, garlic and bell peppers. Cook, covered, until the vegetables are soft, about 5 minutes.

**2.** In a large stainless-steel frying pan, heat the remaining 2 tablespoons oil over moderately high heat. Season the steaks with ½ teaspoon salt and ¼ teaspoon black pepper. Put the steaks in the hot pan and cook until browned, 3 to 4 minutes. Turn and cook until done to medium rare, 3 to 4 minutes longer. Remove.

**3.** Add the bell-pepper mixture, the wine and the remaining ½ teaspoon each salt and black pepper to the large frying pan. Boil until the wine is completely absorbed, about 5 minutes. Serve the steaks topped with the vegetables.

**POUNDING MEAT**

Pounding tenderizes meat and also makes it thinner so it will cook more quickly. Cover the meat with a piece of plastic wrap or waxed paper and then flatten the steak with a traditional meat pounder or the bottom of a heavy frying pan. Or ask your butcher to pound the meat for you.

## wine recommendation

With these steaks, you need a richly flavored, full-bodied red. Take a break from the same old cabernet sauvignon and try a refosco, a robust yet surprisingly sophisticated wine from the extreme northeast corner of Italy.

# steak pizzaiola

*In Italy, the briefly cooked fresh-tomato sauce called* pizzaiola *is traditionally served atop steak. We use sirloin, but if you'd prefer to use flank steak or skirt steak, just reduce the cooking time. The sauce is also good on pasta.*

**PREP TIME**
8 MINUTES

**COOK TIME**
25 MINUTES

**REST TIME**
5 MINUTES

**SERVES 4**

- 4 tablespoons olive oil, more if needed
- 2 cloves garlic, minced
- 1½ pounds tomatoes (about 3), peeled and chopped
- 3 sprigs plus ½ teaspoon chopped fresh oregano, or ¾ teaspoon dried oregano
- ¾ teaspoon salt
- ½ teaspoon fresh-ground black pepper
- 1½ pounds sirloin steak, about 1 inch thick

**1.** In a large saucepan, heat 2 tablespoons of the oil over moderate heat. Add the garlic and cook, stirring, for 1 minute. Add the tomatoes, oregano sprigs or dried oregano, ½ teaspoon of the salt and ¼ teaspoon of the pepper. Reduce the heat and simmer, partially covered, until the sauce thickens, about 15 minutes.

**2.** In a large frying pan, heat the remaining 2 tablespoons oil over moderate heat. Season the steak with the remaining ¼ teaspoon salt and ¼ teaspoon pepper. Cook the steak for 5 minutes. Turn and cook until done to your taste, about 5 minutes longer for medium rare. Remove the steak and let rest in a warm spot for 5 minutes. Cut the steak diagonally into thin slices and top with the warm tomato sauce and the chopped fresh oregano, if using.

## wine recommendation

Barbera—a dry, crisp, medium-bodied red wine from northwestern Italy—is ideal whenever tomatoes and beef come together.

# liver and onions venetian style

*Those who like liver and onions will love this—as will many who don't. With sweet caramelized onions; melting, perfectly cooked liver; and a sprinkling of sage, this earthy dish makes us swoon with pleasure. Serve it over creamy polenta (see Step 2, page 92).*

**PREP TIME**
10 MINUTES

**COOK TIME**
16 MINUTES

**SERVES 4**

- 4 tablespoons olive oil
- 2 tablespoons butter
- 4 onions, sliced thin
- ¾ teaspoon salt
- 1½ pounds ½-inch-thick slices calf's liver, cut into 1½-inch squares
- ¼ teaspoon fresh-ground black pepper
- 6 fresh sage leaves, or ½ teaspoon dried sage

**1.** In a large nonstick frying pan, heat 3 tablespoons of the oil with 1½ tablespoons of the butter over moderately high heat. Add the onions and cook, stirring occasionally, for 10 minutes. Stir in ¼ teaspoon of the salt. Reduce the heat to moderate and cook, stirring frequently, until the onions are well browned, about 5 minutes longer. Remove.

**2.** Sprinkle the liver with the remaining ½ teaspoon salt and the pepper. In the same pan, heat the remaining 1 tablespoon oil and ½ tablespoon butter over high heat. When the pan is very hot, add the liver and sage. Cook, stirring, until just done, 1 to 2 minutes. Remove from the heat, return the onions to the pan and toss.

### HOW TO COOK LIVER

Forget all the bitter, grainy liver you may have had. The way to make liver taste good is primarily a matter of resisting the temptation to overcook it. It should be seared to keep the juices from escaping and should be slightly pink inside, not dingy gray. Use high heat bravely and briefly.

## wine recommendation

Brunello di Montalcino is Tuscany's most exalted wine because it offers a combination of richness, power and elegance unmatched by any other in the region. Serve one here for a sumptuous experience. A more affordable option is Rosso di Montalcino, a sort of scaled-down brunello.

VEAL CHOPS WITH FRESH-TOMATO SAUCE, P. 140

# 6

# *on the grill*

# shrimp with cannellini-bean salad

*Shrimp and sage-scented white beans is a popular Italian combination. Use only high-quality canned beans—Goya is a reliable brand—or your salad will surely be mushy.*

**PREP TIME**
15 MINUTES

**COOK TIME**
5 MINUTES

**SERVES 4**

1½ pounds large shrimp, shelled
½ cup olive oil
2 cloves garlic, minced
½ teaspoon salt
1 small onion, minced
1 tablespoon chopped flat-leaf parsley
1½ tablespoons chopped fresh sage leaves, or 1½ teaspoons dried sage
1 tablespoon wine vinegar
¼ teaspoon fresh-ground black pepper
3⅓ cups drained and rinsed canned cannellini beans (two 15-ounce cans)

**1.** Light the grill or heat the broiler. Thread the shrimp onto four skewers. In a shallow glass dish, combine ¼ cup of the oil with the garlic and ¼ teaspoon of the salt. Add the skewers and turn to coat the shrimp. Set aside.

**2.** In a medium bowl, combine the onion with the remaining ¼ cup oil and ¼ teaspoon salt, the parsley, sage, vinegar and pepper. Gently stir in the beans.

**3.** Grill or broil the shrimp, turning once, until just done, about 5 minutes in all. Serve the shrimp with the bean salad.

**TEST-KITCHEN TIP**

We put the shrimp on skewers before grilling so that they don't fall through the grate. If you don't have metal skewers, the disposable wooden ones work just fine. Soak them in water for ten or fifteen minutes before using them so that they don't burn up. Or you could use a grilling basket.

## wine recommendation

The beans and the shrimp require a white with good body and full flavor. Tocai friulano gives you both, while at the same time contributing a lively acidity that refreshes the palate.

# grilled whole snapper

*Cover the grill while you're cooking the fish to keep the flesh moist and to prevent flare-ups that would burn the bread crumbs. We like to use a grill basket, which helps prevent sticking, but you can cook the fish directly on the grill. Just be sure it's impeccably clean, and turn the fish carefully so you don't lose the crust.*

**PREP TIME**
10 MINUTES

**COOK TIME**
14 MINUTES

**SERVES 4**

2 1¼- to 1½-pound whole red snappers, cleaned and scaled
1 teaspoon salt
2 large sprigs rosemary plus 1 tablespoon chopped fresh rosemary, or 2 teaspoons dried rosemary, crumbled
3 tablespoons olive oil
2 cloves garlic, minced
1 tablespoon dry bread crumbs
Lemon wedges, for serving

**1.** Light the grill. Rinse the fish; dry the surfaces and cavities thoroughly. Cut shallow incisions in a crisscross pattern, about 1 inch apart, in each side of both fish. Season each fish cavity with ⅛ teaspoon of the salt. Put a rosemary sprig in each cavity or rub each with ½ teaspoon dried rosemary. Rub the surface of both fish using 2 tablespoons of the oil, the garlic, the chopped fresh or remaining 1 teaspoon dried rosemary and the remaining ¾ teaspoon salt. Sprinkle the bread crumbs on both sides of each fish. Drizzle both sides with the remaining 1 tablespoon oil.

**2.** Put the fish in a grill basket or onto a very clean grill rack. Cook over moderately high heat for 7 minutes. Turn and grill until golden and just done, about 7 minutes longer. Remove the fish carefully so it doesn't stick.

**3.** Serve the fish on a platter. Run a knife between the flesh and the bones and lift off the fillet. Turn the fish over and repeat. Repeat with the other fish. Pass lemon wedges.

**VARIATION**

**Ⓥ Roasted Whole Snapper**
*Purchase one three-and-a-half-pound snapper instead of two smaller ones. Prepare the fish in the same manner through Step 1, using one-quarter teaspoon salt and both sprigs or one teaspoon rosemary in the cavity. Heat the oven to 450° instead of lighting the grill. Put the fish on a rack in a roasting pan; cook until just done, about twenty minutes. No need to turn the fish while cooking.*

## wine recommendation

Snapper is a delicate fish, and though grilling adds some stronger flavors, you'll be best off with a fairly neutral but crisp white. Orvieto Classico strikes the perfect balance.

# grilled squid salad

*Grill the squid whole and then cut them into slices for this salad. Not only is it easier (no squid rings falling through the grate), but small pieces risk cooking too quickly and becoming rubbery.*

**PREP TIME**
5 MINUTES

**COOK TIME**
5 MINUTES

**SERVES 4**

- 2 pounds cleaned squid
- ¾ cup olive oil
- 1 teaspoon salt
- ¼ cup lemon juice (from about 1 lemon)
- 2 teaspoons wine vinegar
- ¼ teaspoon fresh-ground black pepper
- 3 tablespoons thin-sliced basil leaves
- ½ head green leaf lettuce, torn into bite-size pieces (about 1 quart)
- ¼ cup drained sliced pimientos (2 ounces)
- ½ cup halved and pitted black olives
- 4 scallions including green tops, sliced thin

**1.** Light the grill. In a medium bowl, toss the squid with ¼ cup of the oil and ¾ teaspoon of the salt.

**2.** In a large glass or stainless-steel bowl, combine the lemon juice, vinegar, the remaining ¼ teaspoon salt and the pepper. Stir in the remaining ½ cup oil with a fork. Stir in the basil.

**3.** Grill the squid quickly over high heat, turning once, until just done, 1 to 2 minutes per side. Remove. When cool enough to handle, cut the bodies into ½-inch rings and cut the tentacles in half. Add the squid, lettuce, pimientos, olives and scallions to the dressing and toss.

**VARIATION**

**Ⓥ Shrimp** can replace the squid.
*Toss a pound and a half of large shelled shrimp with the oil and salt, as in Step 1, and grill or broil them until just done, turning once, about five minutes in all.*

## wine recommendation

A light, high-acid wine is a must to stand up to the lemon and vinegar in the dressing here. To highlight the squid, serve a vibrant, fruity pinot grigio from the Alto Adige.

# tuna steaks with lemon caper sauce

*Grilled tuna steaks are one of life's simple pleasures, satisfying even when unadorned. Here they're made better yet with a quick lemon-and-caper sauce, whose pleasant tartness balances the richness of the fish.*

**PREP TIME**
5 MINUTES

**COOK TIME**
8 MINUTES

**SERVES 4**

- 3 tablespoons drained capers
- 1½ tablespoons lemon juice
- ¼ cup chopped fresh parsley
- ¾ teaspoon salt
- ½ teaspoon fresh-ground black pepper
- 8 tablespoons olive oil
- 4 tuna steaks, about ¾ inch thick (about 2 pounds in all)

**1.** Light the grill or heat the broiler. In a small glass or stainless-steel bowl, mash the capers with a fork. Stir in the lemon juice, parsley, ½ teaspoon of the salt and ¼ teaspoon of the pepper and then 6 tablespoons of the oil.

**2.** Coat the tuna with the remaining 2 tablespoons oil. Sprinkle with the remaining ¼ teaspoon each salt and pepper. Grill or broil the tuna for 4 minutes. Turn and cook until done to your taste, 3 to 4 minutes longer for medium rare. Serve the tuna topped with the sauce.

**VARIATIONS**

**V** The lemon-and-caper sauce tastes great on almost any grilled fish. **Swordfish** or **salmon** steaks are especially good choices. Just adjust the cooking time according to the thickness of the fish.

## wine recommendation

Though grilled tuna is superb with pinot noir, here the acidic sauce calls for a white wine. Gavi, Piedmont's cortese-based white, has just the right limelike accents to complement the tangy capers and lemon.

# grilled chicken breasts with lemon and thyme

*A bold mixture of red-pepper flakes, garlic, thyme, lemon juice and olive oil serves as a spicy marinade for bone-in chicken breasts. If you want your chicken spicier still, increase the red pepper or leave the breasts in the marinade for an hour or two.*

**PREP TIME**
5 MINUTES

**COOK TIME**
20 MINUTES

**SERVES 4**

1½ tablespoons lemon juice
¼ teaspoon dried thyme
½ teaspoon dried red-pepper flakes
1 clove garlic, minced
¼ cup olive oil
¼ teaspoon salt
¼ teaspoon fresh-ground black pepper
4 bone-in chicken breasts (about 2¼ pounds in all)

**1.** Light the grill or heat the broiler. In a shallow dish, combine the lemon juice with the thyme, red-pepper flakes, garlic, oil, salt and black pepper. Coat the chicken with the mixture.

**2.** Grill the chicken breasts over moderately high heat or broil them for 8 to 10 minutes. Turn and cook until the chicken is just done, about 10 minutes longer.

## VARIATIONS

**Ⓥ** Try any dried herb you like in place of the thyme. **Marjoram, oregano, rosemary** or **sage** are all good choices.
**Ⓥ** Use **boneless, skinless chicken breasts** instead of bone-in breasts. *Grill them until just done, about five minutes per side over moderately high heat.*
**Ⓥ** Use a **quartered chicken** instead of bone-in breasts. *Cook the breast sections as directed in Step 2 and allow thirteen minutes per side for the leg quarters.*

## wine recommendation

Red pepper can be difficult to pair with wine as it accentuates the bitterness of the alcohol. So, bypass high-alcohol wines and try an herbal, light-bodied sauvignon blanc from Collio.

# chicken salad with gorgonzola, walnuts and figs

*Mild grilled chicken, tender spinach leaves, bitter radicchio, sweet chewy figs, toasted walnuts and creamy tangy Gorgonzola cheese—this combination of contrasting flavors and textures is unforgettable.*

**PREP TIME**
10 MINUTES

**COOK TIME**
15 MINUTES

**SERVES 4**

- 2 cups water
- 6 dried figs
- ⅔ cup walnut halves
- 1⅓ pounds boneless, skinless chicken breasts (about 4)
- 1 tablespoon plus ⅓ cup olive oil
- ½ teaspoon salt
- ½ teaspoon fresh-ground black pepper
- 2 teaspoons chopped fresh rosemary, or ½ teaspoon dried rosemary, crumbled
- 1 head radicchio, torn into 1-inch pieces (about 1½ quarts)
- 12 ounces spinach, large stems removed and leaves washed (about 1½ quarts)
- 1½ tablespoons wine vinegar
- ¼ pound Gorgonzola, crumbled

**1.** Put the water and the figs in a small saucepan. Bring to a boil, turn off the heat and let stand until the figs are plump, 10 to 15 minutes. Drain the figs and cut them in quarters.

**2.** In a small frying pan, toast the walnuts over moderately low heat, stirring frequently, until golden brown, about 5 minutes. Or toast them in a 350° oven for 5 to 10 minutes.

**3.** Light the grill or heat the broiler. Rub the chicken with the 1 tablespoon oil and sprinkle with ¼ teaspoon of the salt, ¼ teaspoon of the pepper and the rosemary. Grill or broil the chicken until just done, about 5 minutes per side. When cool enough to handle, cut into ¼-inch slices.

**4.** Put the radicchio and the spinach in a large bowl. Add the remaining ⅓ cup oil and ¼ teaspoon each salt and pepper and toss. Add the vinegar and toss again. Put the radicchio and spinach on plates. Top with the sliced chicken, and then the Gorgonzola and walnuts. Put some of the figs in the center of each salad.

## wine recommendation

Avoid big reds; walnuts have quite a bit of tannin, which when combined with tannic wines can create overwhelming dryness. A fresh, fruity Bardolino is perfect for this complex salad.

# veal chops with fresh-tomato sauce

*You'll want to use the best summer tomatoes you can find for this uncooked sauce. A touch of balsamic vinegar intensifies both the sweet and sour flavors of the tomatoes. Use a slotted spoon when serving the sauce so the watery liquid that drains off the tomatoes stays in the bowl.*

**PREP TIME**
5 MINUTES

**COOK TIME**
10 MINUTES

**SERVES 4**

5½ tablespoons olive oil
¼ cup red wine
¾ teaspoon salt
Fresh-ground black pepper
2 cloves garlic, smashed
4 veal loin chops, about 1 inch thick (about 3 pounds in all)
1¼ pounds vine-ripened tomatoes (about 4), chopped
1½ tablespoons chopped mixed fresh herbs, such as parsley, basil and chives
½ teaspoon balsamic vinegar

**1.** Light the grill or heat the broiler. In a shallow dish, combine 4 tablespoons of the oil with the wine, ½ teaspoon of the salt, ¼ teaspoon pepper and the garlic. Add the veal chops and turn to coat.

**2.** In a medium glass or stainless-steel bowl, combine the tomatoes with the remaining ¼ teaspoon salt, the remaining 1½ tablespoons oil, the herbs, vinegar and a large pinch of pepper.

**3.** Grill the chops over high heat or broil them for 4 to 5 minutes. Turn and cook until just done, 4 to 5 minutes longer. Serve the veal chops topped with the tomato sauce.

**VARIATION**

**Ⓥ** If you're in a rush or tomatoes are out of season, **skip the tomato sauce.** The chops are perfectly fine on their own.

## wine recommendation

Don't bury the veal and its light sauce under a big, tannic wine. Dolcetto, with its fresh cherry and herb flavors and crisp, refreshing bite, is a much better choice.

# lamb chops with garlic and olive oil

*Tender rib chops take only a few minutes per side to cook but are elegant enough to serve to company. Coat them with just the garlic and oil, or try one of our herb variations.*

**PREP TIME**
5 MINUTES

**COOK TIME**
10 MINUTES

**SERVES 4**

- 6 tablespoons olive oil
- 2 cloves garlic, minced
- ½ teaspoon salt
- ¼ teaspoon fresh-ground black pepper
- 8 lamb rib chops, about 1 inch thick (about 2¾ pounds in all)

**1.** Light the grill or heat the broiler. In a shallow dish, combine 4 tablespoons of the oil with the garlic, salt and pepper. Add the lamb chops and turn to coat.

**2.** Grill the lamb chops over high heat or broil them for 5 minutes, basting with the remaining 2 tablespoons oil. Turn and cook until done, about 5 minutes longer.

**VARIATIONS**

Ⓥ Add four teaspoons chopped fresh **rosemary** to the garlic and oil mixture.
Ⓥ Add three tablespoons chopped fresh **sage** and an additional tablespoon olive oil to the garlic and oil mixture.
Ⓥ Use lamb **loin chops** instead of rib chops.

**TEST-KITCHEN TIPS**

When grilling quick-cooking items such as chops, turn them only once. If you leave the meat alone for a few minutes, it will have a chance to form a nice brown crust. If you move it too soon, the meat will stick, and you'll pull off the incipient crust. Once that brown edge forms, the meat is easy to move.

When you do turn the meat, use tongs or a spatula. Never poke a fork into the meat or the precious juices will escape.

## wine recommendation

Grilled lamb chops are the perfect foil for the rich cassis and herbal flavors of cabernet sauvignon. Your best bet here is a so-called super Tuscan. Though the most famous wines, such as Sassicaia and Tignanello, fetch astronomical prices, many excellent values can also be found.

# florentine beefsteak

*One of the simplest yet most succulent dishes of Florence is the renowned* bistecca alla fiorentina. *Thick T-bone steaks of the highest quality and a very hot grill are the keys to success. Italians cook the steak rare and often douse it with a healthy squeeze of lemon. The combination of rich, red meat and tart juice is nothing short of exceptional. Do try it.*

**COOK TIME**
12 MINUTES

**SERVES 4**

2  T-bone steaks, 1½ inches thick (about 4 pounds in all)
1  tablespoon olive oil
2  teaspoons salt
½  teaspoon fresh-ground black pepper
Lemon wedges, for serving

**1.** Light the grill. Rub the steaks with the oil and sprinkle with the salt and pepper.

**2.** Grill the steaks over high heat for 6 minutes. Turn and cook until done to your taste, about 6 minutes longer for rare. Serve with lemon wedges.

**STEAK CHOICE**

If you like, use **porterhouse steaks** instead of T-bones. Both of these bone-in steaks come from the short loin section of the animal. The bone separates the steak into strip loin and tenderloin sections. The strip loin has more flavor and the tenderloin is tenderer. Porterhouse steaks have more tenderloin and T-bones have a larger strip loin section. Choose according to your preference.

## wine recommendation

There's nothing like a great steak to showcase a special, and if possible older, Barolo or Barbaresco. Made from the nebbiolo grape, these wines develop fabulously complex dried cherry, eucalyptus, floral and truffle flavors along with a silky texture. Both have power to spare, but Barbaresco is more elegant.

ROAST CHICKEN WITH BUTTERNUT SQUASH, P. 152

# *in the oven*

# roasted swordfish and potatoes with caper mayonnaise

*Ready-made mayonnaise is a bit sweet but tastes fine when balanced by acidic ingredients such as the vinegar and capers here. It's good with both the fish and potatoes.*

**PREP TIME**
6 MINUTES

**COOK TIME**
25 MINUTES

**SERVES 4**

1½ pounds boiling potatoes (about 4), cut into ½-inch pieces
½ cup olive oil
5 cloves garlic, chopped
½ teaspoon salt
½ teaspoon fresh-ground black pepper
4 swordfish steaks, about 1 inch thick (about 2 pounds in all)
1 teaspoon chopped fresh rosemary, or ½ teaspoon dried rosemary, crumbled
1 cup mayonnaise
2 tablespoons chopped fresh parsley
2 tablespoons drained chopped capers
1 teaspoon wine vinegar

**1.** Heat the oven to 400°. In a large roasting pan, toss the potatoes with ¼ cup of the oil, half the garlic and ¼ teaspoon each salt and pepper. Roast the potatoes in the oven until tender and browned, stirring twice, about 25 minutes.

**2.** Meanwhile, on a rimmed baking sheet, coat the swordfish with the remaining ¼ cup oil, garlic, ¼ teaspoon each salt and pepper and the rosemary. When the potatoes have been roasting for 15 minutes, put the swordfish in the oven and roast until just white throughout, about 10 minutes.

**3.** In a small bowl, combine the mayonnaise with the parsley, capers and vinegar. Serve the roasted swordfish and potatoes with the caper mayonnaise.

**VARIATIONS**

Ⓥ Try **tuna**, **salmon** or **codfish** steaks instead of the swordfish. Fillets will also be good in this recipe, but you'll need to cut down on the cooking time. If you do, be sure the potatoes still cook for twenty-five minutes. Just put the fish in later.

## wine recommendation

Though not a typical Italian wine, pinot noir is superb with swordfish. There are some tasty pinot noirs from the Alto Adige and Friuli, which you'll find under the Italian name pinot nero.

# roast chicken with lemon, oregano and vermouth

*Simple roasted chicken parts are perfect for a weeknight meal. You'll have just enough concentrated jus to drizzle a little over each oregano-scented piece.*

PREP TIME
8 MINUTES

COOK TIME
35 MINUTES

**SERVES 4**

- 1 chicken (3 to 3½ pounds), cut into 8 pieces
- 4 teaspoons olive oil
- 1½ teaspoons dried oregano
- 2 tablespoons dry vermouth or white wine
- 1 teaspoon lemon juice
- ¼ teaspoon salt
- ⅛ teaspoon fresh-ground black pepper
- 2 tablespoons water

**1.** Heat the oven to 375°. Coat the chicken with 3 teaspoons of the oil. Put the pieces, skin-side up, in a large roasting pan. Sprinkle the chicken with the oregano, 1 tablespoon of the vermouth, the lemon juice, salt and pepper. Drizzle the remaining 1 teaspoon oil over the top.

**2.** Cook the chicken until the breasts are just done, about 25 minutes. Remove the breasts and wings and continue to cook the drumsticks and thighs until done, about 5 minutes longer.

**3.** Heat the broiler. Remove the roasting pan from the oven; return the breasts and wings to the pan. Broil the chicken until golden brown, about 2 minutes. Remove the chicken from the pan.

**4.** Pour off the fat from the roasting pan. Set the pan over moderate heat and add the remaining 1 tablespoon vermouth and the water. Bring to a boil, scraping the bottom of the pan to dislodge any brown bits. Boil until reduced to approximately 2 tablespoons. Add any accumulated juices from the chicken. Spoon the sauce over the chicken.

**VARIATION**

- If you prefer **all white or dark meat,** use four bone-in breasts, eight drumsticks or eight thighs instead of assorted pieces.
  *Cook the breasts for twenty-five minutes or the legs for thirty minutes.*

## wine recommendation

This rustic, herbal roast chicken is best served with a full-bodied and strongly flavored white wine. Look to the south, where the earthy, richly nutty Greco di Tufo is found. Although virtually unknown, it's one of Italy's great whites.

# roast chicken with butternut squash

*Chicken quarters roasted with golden squash and sage are nice for a chilly autumn evening. To help the squash to brown evenly, be sure to spoon off the fat from the roasting pan after removing the breasts. This is a case where less is more: A thin layer of fat will brown the vegetable better than a quarter-inch of it.*

PREP TIME
10 MINUTES

COOK TIME
35 MINUTES

**SERVES 4**

- 1   chicken (3 to 3½ pounds), quartered
- 3   tablespoons olive oil
- ¾   teaspoon salt
- ¼   teaspoon fresh-ground black pepper
- 1   small butternut squash (about 2¼ pounds), peeled and cut into 1-inch cubes
- 1   teaspoon dried sage
- 3   tablespoons water

**1.** Heat the oven to 450°. Coat the chicken quarters with 1 tablespoon of the oil, ½ teaspoon of the salt and ⅛ teaspoon of the pepper. Arrange the chicken quarters, skin-side up, in a large roasting pan. Toss the cubes of butternut squash with the remaining 2 tablespoons oil, ¼ teaspoon salt and ⅛ teaspoon pepper, and the sage. Add the cubes of squash to the roasting pan.

**2.** Cook, stirring the squash occasionally, until the chicken breasts are just done, about 20 minutes. Remove the pan from the oven and remove the breasts from the pan. Tilt the roasting pan and spoon off most of the fat from the pan. Return the pan to the oven. Continue cooking until the chicken legs and the squash are done, about 10 minutes longer. Remove the chicken and squash from the pan.

**3.** Pour off the fat from the roasting pan. Set the pan over moderate heat and add the water. Bring to a boil, scraping the bottom of the pan to dislodge any brown bits. Boil until reduced to approximately 2 tablespoons. Add any accumulated juices from the chicken. Spoon the sauce over the chicken.

**VARIATIONS**

- Ⓥ Instead of the butternut, use your favorite winter squash, such as **acorn** or **Hubbard**—or, to be really Italian, try **pumpkin.**
- Ⓥ Replace the chicken quarters with halved **Cornish hens.**

## wine recommendation

This winter-weight dish calls for a simple but robust red, and the sturdy Montepulciano d'Abruzzo, with its roasted-berry flavor, is just right. Best of all, it's among the least expensive of all Italian reds.

# baked pork chops with swiss chard

*There's no need to brown the pork chops first; just pop them in the oven. As the chops bake, their juices will seep into the Swiss chard, flavoring the entire dish.*

**PREP TIME**
5 MINUTES

**COOK TIME**
20 MINUTES

**REST TIME**
5 MINUTES

**SERVES 4**

 1  pound Swiss chard, stems
    removed, leaves washed
    and cut crosswise into 1-inch
    pieces
 3  tablespoons olive oil
 ½  teaspoon salt
Fresh-ground black pepper
 4  pork chops, about 1 inch thick
    (about 2 pounds in all)
1½ tablespoons grated Parmesan
 2  ounces grated fontina
    (about ½ cup)

**1.** Heat the oven to 450°. Oil a 7½-by-11½-inch baking dish. In a medium bowl, toss the Swiss chard with 1 tablespoon of the oil, ¼ teaspoon of the salt and ¼ teaspoon pepper. Put the chard in the baking dish.

**2.** Rub the pork chops with 1 tablespoon of the oil, the remaining ¼ teaspoon salt and ⅛ teaspoon pepper. Put the pork chops on top of the Swiss chard. Drizzle the remaining 1 tablespoon oil over the chard, around the pork chops. Sprinkle the Parmesan and fontina over the chard, around the chops. Bake until the chops are just done, about 18 minutes. Let stand 5 minutes before serving.

### SWISS CHARD

You can use either green or red Swiss chard for this dish. You'll want to rinse the leaves thoroughly before cooking, but don't dry them. The moisture will help keep the chard from drying out during cooking.

## wine recommendation

Wines based on the sangiovese grape work particularly well with pork chops. Try a Vino Nobile di Montepulciano, similar to Chianti but richer, earthier and more powerful.

# portobello-mushroom and red-pepper pizza

*Depending on the size of the appetites around your house, this substantial pizza with its meaty portobello mushrooms serves two very hungry people or four if it's accompanied by a big salad. If you don't have fresh basil, stir some pesto into the peppers and mushrooms before putting them on the pizza.*

**PREP TIME**
10 MINUTES

**COOK TIME**
45 MINUTES

**MAKES ONE 14-INCH PIZZA**

- 6 tablespoons olive oil
- 2 red bell peppers, cut into thin slices
- 1½ pounds portobello mushrooms, stems removed, caps cut into ¼-inch slices
- 1 teaspoon salt
- 1 pound store-bought or homemade pizza dough
- 3 cloves garlic, minced
- ¼ teaspoon fresh-ground black pepper
- ¾ cup lightly packed basil leaves, chopped
- ½ pound fresh salted mozzarella, cut into ¼-inch cubes
- ½ cup grated Parmesan

**1.** Heat the oven to 450°. In a large frying pan, heat 3 tablespoons of the oil over moderately high heat. Put the peppers in the pan and cook, stirring occasionally, for 10 minutes. Add the mushrooms and the salt and cook, stirring occasionally, until the mushrooms are golden, about 10 minutes more.

**2.** Meanwhile, oil a 14-inch pizza pan or large baking sheet. Press the pizza dough onto the pan in an approximately 14-inch round or 9-by-13-inch rectangle.

**3.** Spread the peppers and mushrooms on the pizza crust. Bake for 12 minutes. Sprinkle on the garlic, black pepper and basil. Top with the mozzarella and then with the Parmesan. Drizzle with the remaining 3 tablespoons oil. Bake until the cheese is bubbling and beginning to brown, about 10 to 15 minutes longer.

## wine recommendation

Most dolcetto comes from two major centers in Piedmont: Asti, which produces lighter and sharper wines, and Alba, whose wines are rounder and fuller. Try the Alba version with this pizza.

# eggplant, pesto and goat-cheese pizza

*Tangy goat cheese, sharp Parmesan, tender sautéed eggplant and bold pesto cover a mouthwatering pizza. As with the preceding recipe, this one makes a hearty fourteen-inch pizza; you be the judge whether it serves two or four.*

**PREP TIME**
10 MINUTES

**COOK TIME**
1 HOUR

**MAKES ONE 14-INCH PIZZA**

7½ tablespoons olive oil, or more as needed
 1 1½- to 2-pound eggplant, cut into ¼-inch slices
 ¾ teaspoon salt
 1 pound store-bought or homemade pizza dough
 3 cloves garlic, minced
 ½ teaspoon fresh-ground black pepper
 6 ounces mild goat cheese, such as Montrachet, cut into ¼-inch slices
 ½ cup grated Parmesan
 ½ cup store-bought or homemade pesto

**1.** Heat the oven to 450°. In a large nonstick frying pan, heat 2½ tablespoons of the oil over moderately high heat. Season the eggplant with the salt. Fry one-third of the eggplant, turning, until golden, about 10 minutes. Remove. Repeat in two more batches with the remaining oil, using more if needed, and eggplant.

**2.** Meanwhile, oil a 14-inch pizza pan or large baking sheet. Press the pizza dough onto the pan in an approximately 14-inch round or 9-by-13-inch rectangle.

**3.** Arrange the eggplant slices on the pizza crust. Sprinkle the garlic and pepper over the top. Bake for 12 minutes. Put the slices of goat cheese on the pizza, sprinkle with the Parmesan and then dot with the pesto. Bake until the cheese begins to turn golden, about 15 minutes.

**PIZZA DOUGH**

Most supermarkets carry pizza dough; look for it in the refrigerator section. Another possibility is to ask for it at your favorite pizza restaurant. Many places are willing to sell it by the pound.

## wine recommendation

Sauvignon blanc is a remarkably versatile wine, and it's particularly delicious with goat cheese and basil. Once again, northeastern Italy is the place to look for these fresh, bracing wines.

# potato pie with tomato and fontina

*It looks, smells and tastes like pizza, with one delicious difference: The crust is made of mashed potatoes. You'll have to use a fork to eat this pie, since the slices aren't sturdy enough to hold in your hand.*

**PREP TIME**
10 MINUTES

**COOK TIME**
50 MINUTES

**SERVES 4**

2½ pounds baking potatoes (about 5), peeled and halved
 1 28-ounce can tomatoes, drained and chopped fine (about 1 cup)
1¼ teaspoons salt
 4 tablespoons olive oil
Fresh-ground black pepper
 ¾ pound grated fontina (about 3 cups)
 3 cloves garlic, minced
 5 anchovy fillets, minced
 2 teaspoons dried oregano
 ⅓ cup grated Parmesan

**1.** Heat the oven to 450°. Put the potatoes in a medium saucepan of salted water. Bring to a boil, reduce the heat and simmer until tender, about 20 minutes. Meanwhile, put the tomatoes in a strainer set over a medium bowl. Toss with ¾ teaspoon of the salt and let drain for 20 minutes.

**2.** Drain the potatoes and push them through a food mill, ricer or strainer back into the saucepan. Cook over moderately low heat, stirring, until the potato starts to stick to the pan, about 5 minutes. Stir in 2 tablespoons of the oil, the remaining ½ teaspoon salt and a pinch of pepper. Remove from the heat.

**3.** Oil a large baking sheet. Spread the potato mixture onto the baking sheet, forming two 6-by-11-inch rectangles. Top the potato with the fontina, leaving a ¼-inch border. Sprinkle the garlic and anchovies over the cheese. Top with the drained tomatoes followed by the oregano and Parmesan. Drizzle with the remaining 2 tablespoons oil. Bake the potato pies in the lower third of the oven until the cheese is bubbling and the edges are golden brown, about 25 minutes.

## wine recommendation

Barbera and dolcetto are the everyday workhorse wines of Piedmont. The more acidic and fruitier barbera is the better choice for dishes with a lot of tomatoes.

HONEY-BAKED FIGS WITH
ICE CREAM, P. 170

# 8

# *desserts*

# pineapple carpaccio with lemon sorbet and candied zest

*Here's a refreshing dessert that looks and tastes spectacular. If you can find one, try a pineapple labeled "gold"; this hybrid is always lusciously sweet.*

**PREP TIME**
15 MINUTES

**COOK TIME**
25 MINUTES

**SERVES 4**

2 oranges
2¼ cups water
¾ cup sugar
1 pineapple, chilled, peeled and halved lengthwise
1 pint lemon sorbet
4 sprigs mint, for garnish (optional)

**1.** Using a vegetable peeler, cut the zest from one of the oranges in wide strips and then into matchstick strips. Put the zest in a medium saucepan with the water and sugar. Simmer until the zest is translucent and tender and the liquid is reduced to approximately ⅔ cup, about 25 minutes. Strain out the zest, reserving both the syrup and the zest. Squeeze ¾ cup juice from the oranges, strain into the syrup and chill in the refrigerator.

**2.** Core each half of the pineapple by making a diagonal cut on one side of the core with a long serrated knife. Make a diagonal cut on the other side of the core, forming a V. Remove the core. Turn the halves over and cut the pineapple crosswise into ⅛-inch slices. Arrange the slices on four plates in concentric circles.

**3.** Pour the orange syrup over the pineapple slices. Put a scoop of sorbet on top of the pineapple and the candied zest over the sorbet. Garnish with the mint.

# espresso granita with whipped cream

*Top the granita with a hefty portion of whipped cream; you'll need the mild sweetness of the cream to balance the strong espresso. If you're cutting down on caffeine, you can use decaffeinated espresso beans instead of regular.*

**PREP TIME**
10 MINUTES

**CHILL AND FREEZE TIME**
1 HOUR

**MAKES 1 PINT GRANITA**

- 2 **cups ground espresso beans**
- 3 **cups water**
- ¼ **cup plus 4 teaspoons sugar, more to taste**
- ⅔ **cup heavy cream**

**1.** Using an espresso machine, make coffee with the ground espresso and the water. You should have 1¾ cups strong espresso. Alternatively, make 1¾ cups espresso using a French press or drip coffee maker. Add the ¼ cup sugar and stir until dissolved. Taste the espresso and add more sugar if necessary. Chill in the refrigerator, or, to hasten the process, pour the espresso into a stainless-steel bowl, set it in a larger bowl filled with ice and stir the coffee until cold.

**2.** Pour the chilled coffee into two 9-by-9-inch stainless-steel pans. Freeze for 15 minutes. Stir well and return the pans to the freezer. Continue freezing, stirring every 10 minutes, until the granita is completely frozen, about 40 minutes in all.

**3.** In a medium bowl, using a handheld electric mixer, beat the cream with the remaining 4 teaspoons sugar until the cream holds soft peaks when the beaters are lifted. Scoop the granita into chilled serving bowls and top with the whipped cream.

**GRANITA TIPS**

For extra speed, buy the espresso ready-made from a coffee shop.

You can put the warm espresso directly into the freezer, but it will take much longer to freeze.

Granita will freeze faster in a metal pan, but you can use Pyrex; just allow more time. Or freeze the liquid in metal bowls.

Stir the granita with a fork to get a nice fine grain.

Granita melts quickly, so serve it in bowls or glasses that have been chilled in the freezer.

# lemon and rosemary granita

*An icy treat for a warm summer evening, this granita gets an unexpected boost from the bold flavor of rosemary. You can put the hot lemon mixture directly into the freezer rather than chilling it first, but the freezing time will be longer.*

**PREP TIME**
5 MINUTES

**COOK TIME**
5 MINUTES

**INFUSE, CHILL AND FREEZE TIME**
1 HOUR
30 MINUTES

**MAKES ABOUT 1 QUART GRANITA**

3 cups water
1 cup plus 2 tablespoons sugar
4 4-inch sprigs fresh rosemary, or 3 tablespoons dried rosemary, crumbled
4 ½-by-3-inch strips lemon zest
1¼ cups lemon juice (from about 5 lemons)
3 tablespoons Grand Marnier or other orange liqueur

**1.** In a medium saucepan, combine the water, sugar, rosemary and lemon zest. Bring to a simmer, stirring constantly. Remove from the heat, cover and let infuse for 10 minutes.

**2.** In a large glass or stainless-steel bowl, combine the lemon juice and Grand Marnier. Strain the rosemary syrup into the lemon juice and stir to combine. Chill in the refrigerator or, to hasten the process, pour the lemon mixture into a stainless-steel bowl, set it in a larger bowl filled with ice and stir until cold.

**3.** Pour the chilled lemon mixture into two 9-by-9-inch stainless-steel pans. Freeze for 15 minutes. Stir well and return the pans to the freezer. Continue freezing, stirring every 15 minutes, until the granita is completely frozen, about 1 hour in all. When ready to serve, scoop the granita into chilled bowls or stemmed glasses.

# honey-baked figs with ice cream

*Use purplish-black Mission figs, green-skinned Calimyrnas or both for this great-tasting dessert. Give the figs a gentle squeeze to check for ripeness; they should be quite soft.*

**PREP TIME**
6 MINUTES

**COOK TIME**
10 MINUTES

**SERVES 4**

12 fresh figs
1½ teaspoons olive oil
4 teaspoons honey
2 tablespoons cold butter,
cut into 12 pieces
2 tablespoons water
1 pint vanilla ice cream

**1.** Heat the oven to 425°. Cut the stems off the figs. Rub the oil over the figs and put them in a baking pan, stem-side up. Cut a cross in the top of each fig, cutting almost to the bottom.

**2.** Drizzle the honey over the figs. Top each one with a piece of the butter. Bake the figs until they open up like flowers, 8 to 10 minutes. Remove the pan from the oven.

**3.** Put the figs on plates, add the water to the pan, return the pan to the oven for 1 minute and then stir to make a sauce. Drizzle the sauce over the warm figs and serve with a scoop of vanilla ice cream on the side.

**VARIATIONS**

**V** Sprinkle one-half cup chopped **walnuts** or **pistachios** over the figs after the first seven minutes of cooking.

# ricotta ice cream with honey and almonds

*For an unusual but exceptionally easy dessert, soften a pint of vanilla ice cream, mix it with ricotta and honey and then refreeze it. You'll want to use a premium brand of ice cream, since the quality of each ingredient is very apparent in this simple dessert.*

**PREP TIME**
10 MINUTES

**COOK TIME**
5–10 MINUTES

**FREEZE TIME**
1 HOUR

**MAKES 1½ PINTS ICE CREAM**

¾ cup sliced almonds
1 pint vanilla ice cream
1½ cups ricotta cheese
½ cup honey

**1.** In a small frying pan, toast the almonds over moderately low heat, stirring frequently, until golden brown, about 5 minutes. Or toast them in a 350° oven for 5 to 10 minutes. Let cool completely.

**2.** Put a large metal bowl in the freezer. Let the ice cream stand at room temperature until just beginning to soften but still frozen. In a food processor, puree the ricotta and honey until smooth.

**3.** Remove the bowl from the freezer and put the ice cream in it. Stir until smooth. Stir in the ricotta mixture. Transfer the ice-cream mixture to a shallow stainless-steel pan and then return it to the freezer, covered, until firm enough to scoop, about 1 hour. Serve the ice cream topped with the toasted almonds.

# baked peaches with almond paste

*Stuff ripe, juicy peach halves with pureed almond paste and then bake them until tender and golden. Puree the almond mixture ahead of time if you like, but wait until the last minute to cut and stuff the peaches, or they'll turn brown.*

**PREP TIME**
5 MINUTES

**COOK TIME**
25 MINUTES

**SERVES 4**

4  peaches, halved and pitted
6  ounces almond paste
   (about ½ cup)
3  tablespoons hot water
1  teaspoon lemon juice
1½ teaspoons cold butter,
   cut into 8 pieces

**1.** Heat the oven to 400°. Put a rack on a baking sheet and then put the peaches on the rack, skin-side down.

**2.** In a food processor, puree the almond paste, water and lemon juice. Spoon the almond mixture into the centers of the peaches. Top each mound of almond paste with a piece of the butter.

**3.** Bake in the lower third of the oven until the peaches are tender and the almond paste is golden brown, about 25 minutes. Serve warm.

### PEELING THE PEACHES

Peel the peaches or not, as you like. The blush on the skin is pretty, but during taste tests most of us pulled off the peel and pushed it to the side of the plate.

### ALMOND PASTE

Almond paste is simply a combination of ground almonds and sugar. It's available in supermarkets, usually in the baking aisle, and comes in both cans and tubes.

# zabaglione with strawberries

*Here we serve the zabaglione hot when it's just made, but if you want to prepare the dish ahead of time, mix the zabaglione with whipped cream and refrigerate it as described in the first variation below.*

**PREP TIME**
5 MINUTES

**COOK TIME**
10 MINUTES

**SERVES 4**

8   large egg yolks, at room temperature
¾   cup dry marsala
½   cup sugar
1   pint strawberries, sliced

**1.** Put the egg yolks, the marsala and then the sugar into a large stainless-steel bowl. Set the bowl over a large saucepan filled with 1 inch of barely simmering water. Using a handheld electric mixer on low speed or a whisk, beat the egg-yolk mixture until it is hot and the mixture forms a ribbon when the beaters are lifted, 5 to 8 minutes. Don't cook the zabaglione for too long, or it will curdle.

**2.** Put the strawberries in stemmed glasses or bowls. Top with the hot zabaglione and either serve the dessert immediately or refrigerate it for up to an hour.

### VARIATIONS

**V** For a zabaglione that will last up to six hours in the refrigerator, add **whipped cream.**
*Beat half a cup of heavy cream just until it holds firm peaks. When the zabaglione is done, remove the bowl from the heat and continue beating until it's cool. Fold the cooled zabaglione into the whipped cream. Put the strawberries in bowls, top with the zabaglione and refrigerate.*

**V** Substitute **blueberries, raspberries** or sliced **peaches** for the strawberries.

### TEST-KITCHEN TIP

What you need to make zabaglione is, in effect, a double boiler that's wide enough to accommodate an electric mixer. This is easy to rig up with a heatproof bowl set over a saucepan.

# cherries poached in red wine with mascarpone cream

*Thick mascarpone cheese mixed with honey makes a luscious topping for poached cherries. You can serve the dessert either warm or cold. We love it both ways.*

**PREP TIME**
8 MINUTES

**COOK TIME**
5 MINUTES

**SERVES 4**

2¼ cups red wine
1 cup sugar
1 1-by-3-inch strip orange zest
2 pounds sweet cherries, halved and pitted
1 cup mascarpone cheese
2½ tablespoons honey

**1.** In a medium stainless-steel saucepan, combine the wine, sugar and orange zest. Bring to a simmer over moderately high heat. Add the cherries and bring back to a simmer. Reduce the heat and simmer, partially covered, until the cherries are just tender, about 5 minutes. Pour into a glass or stainless-steel bowl so the cherries don't overcook.

**2.** In a small bowl, combine the mascarpone with the honey. Remove the strip of orange zest from the cherries. Serve the warm cherries and syrup in bowls or stemmed glasses, topped with a large dollop of the mascarpone cream.

**VARIATIONS**

**V** The warm cherries and poaching liquid are great alone—without the mascarpone cream—or with **whipped cream.**

**V** Serve the mascarpone cream with cut up **fresh fruit** or **mixed berries** instead of with the poached cherries.

# *essential*
# ITALIAN INGREDIENTS

### Anchovies

Give anchovies a chance; they give a dish tremendous depth of flavor. Use salt-packed, jarred or canned anchovies, or even anchovy paste—whichever form you prefer. Half a teaspoon of anchovy paste equals two flat anchovy fillets.

### Bread Crumbs

Bread crumbs, either dry or fresh, are used as a coating for fried meat and fish and as a topping for pasta and crusty vegetable gratins. Making fresh bread crumbs is simple: Put pieces of bread in the food processor and give it a whir.

### Broth

Italians generally make broth from a combination of meat and chicken. However, we developed all of the recipes in this book using canned low-sodium chicken broth. You can substitute regular for low-sodium broth, if you prefer; just cut back on the salt in the recipe. Of course, if you keep homemade chicken stock or meat broth in the freezer, by all means use it.

### Capers

These tart Mediterranean flower buds add piquancy to a dish. Since they come bottled in a vinegary brine, you'll want to drain them before use. We use small nonpareil capers in these recipes; if you use larger ones, just chop them first.

### Cornmeal

Cornmeal is ground from dried kernels of yellow or white corn. Its texture ranges from powdery to quite coarse; you'll want to use a medium- or coarse-textured cornmeal for making polenta. We don't recommend instant polenta, which often has seasonings and dried vegetables added to it.

### Garlic

Although garlic is commonly associated with Italian cooking, use just enough of it to flavor a dish, not enough to kill a vampire. Keep in mind that the size of garlic cloves varies tremendously; when we call for one minced or chopped clove, we expect you to get about three-quarters of a teaspoon. When cooking with garlic, be careful to never let it burn or it will taste bitter.

### Herbs

Italian cooking makes frequent use of basil, bay leaves, marjoram, oregano, flat-leaf parsley, rosemary, sage and thyme. Use only fresh basil, parsley and marjoram; they don't dry well. In fact, basil is best not only fresh but raw, added to warm dishes only at the last minute. Besides these three, the other herbs retain their character when dried, so you can use them confidently in either form.

## Lemon Juice

Fresh-squeezed lemon juice adds bright acidity to dressings, marinades, grilled meats and fish and cooked or raw vegetables. Not only is lemon juice an ingredient in many recipes, but lemon wedges are frequently served alongside the dish so the diner can add a final burst of flavor and aroma just before eating.

## Olive Oil

As a cornerstone of the Italian kitchen, olive oil appears in virtually every part of the meal. Choose an extra-virgin oil, which comes from the first cold pressing of the olives, to use in both salads and in cooking. Olive oil doesn't age well; store it in a cool, dry place and try to use it within a year. When the oil loses its bright, fresh scent and starts to smell like cardboard, it's rancid.

## Olives

If your store doesn't sell olives from big, open barrels, opt for the kind in jars. The canned version gives you only the slightest hint of what a good olive might taste like.

## Pasta, Dry

With hundreds of shapes to choose from, dry pasta is a lifesaver when you want to make dinner quickly. Flour-and-water pasta, such as spaghetti and macaroni, is virtually always bought dried, even in Italy. Egg pasta (all the flat types, like fettuccine and pappardelle) can be glorious fresh, but unless you're going to make your own—definitely not a quick task—dried is a better bet than most store-bought fresh, which tends to be mushy, flavorless or both, as well as more expensive.

## Pepper

There's nothing like fresh-ground black pepper. If you've been using preground, buy a pepper mill, fill it and give it a grind. You'll never look back.

## Pine Nuts

Pine nuts come from pine cones. The pignoli from Italy, Spain and Portugal are more desirable than the nuts from China (which have a stronger pine flavor), but they're also considerably more expensive. The Chinese ones are fine for most cooking.

## Porcini Mushrooms, Dried

Since fresh porcini mushrooms are seasonal and quite expensive, the dried version is a handy alternative. Dried porcini are available in small packages weighing about an ounce, and they keep indefinitely. Their flavor is concentrated and intense. Put the mushrooms in warm water to reconstitute them before using. After a soak, remove the mushrooms from the liquid, rinse and dry them before continuing with the recipe. Save the soaking liquid to enhance risottos, soups and sauces.

## Prosciutto

The remarkable balance of sweetness and saltiness gives prosciutto great appeal. Prosciutto is pork that has been salt cured and air-dried; it is never smoked. Due to its full, satisfying flavor, a little goes a long way in cooking.

## Rice, Arborio

Arborio rice appears in Italian soups and boiled rice dishes, but plays its major role in risotto. The short, stubby grains contain loads of starch, which is released into the broth during cooking. Risotto makes its own sauce of thickened, creamy broth.

## Tomatoes

If you plan to use fresh tomatoes, be sure they are vine ripened to a full red. If you can't find good ones, use high-quality canned, peeled plum tomatoes. Many domestic brands, as well as those imported from the San Marzano region in Italy, are excellent and are available in supermarkets.

## Tuna, Canned

Tuna packed in olive oil is more moist and flavorful than water-packed, perfect for salads, sauces and antipasti. You can drain off the oil from the tuna or add it to what you're cooking; the tuna-impregnated olive oil will heighten the taste of the dish.

## Vinegar

In general, use either red- or white-wine vinegar for cooking and for salads. Balsamic vinegar, which can range from heavenly to horrible, is added sparingly to dishes toward the end of cooking, or combined with other vinegars for green salads. Look for balsamic vinegar from Modena, aged if possible.

## Wine

Wine is nearly as essential to Italian cooking as it is to French. Often a bit of a bottle is used for braising meat or making a simple pan sauce, and then the remainder is served with the meal. Or the end of yesterday's bottle can be put to good use in today's cooking. Dry vermouth can be used as an alternative to dry white wine.

# INDEX